TRAINING THE
POINTER-RETRIEVER
GUNDOG

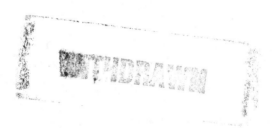

Michael Brander

SWAN·HILL
PRESS

Copyright © 1991 by Michael Brander

First published in the UK by Pelham Books in 1983.
This edition first published by Swan Hill Press 1991.

British Library Cataloguing in Publication Data
Brander, Michael, *1924 –*
    Training the pointer – retriever gundog.
    1. Dogs. training
    I. Title
    736.752
    ISBN 1 85310 238 5

Printed in England by Livesey Ltd., Shrewsbury.

Swan Hill Press

An Imprint of Airlife Publishing Ltd.
101 Longden Road, Shrewsbury SY3 9EB, England.

Contents

Illustrations

PHOTO CREDIT

All the photographs are by Glyn Satterley.

Foreword

I have now been closely associated with hunting, pointing and retrieving dogs for over forty years. I learned from my first German Shorthaired Pointer dog, Max, how they should work and he was largely responsible for my first book on training hunting dogs, *The Roughshooter's Dog*, which was published in 1957, then the only book in English on the subject. Since then I have learned a good deal from his successors and I hope to go on learning a lot more. It has been interesting in the intervening years judging all the hunting breeds in field trials and even more so shooting over them in the field. It may sound surprising, but it is nonetheless true, that a labrador trained on the lines I suggested in that book proved as good a pointer-retriever as almost any I have seen.

The Roughshooter's Dog went out of print in 1980 and in 1983 I was commissioned to write this book as a complementary work on training, incorporating what I had learned from my dogs over the intervening years. This edition is now being re-published with entirely new illustrations, but the words I wrote in 1957, which are also repeated in the latest edition of *The Roughshooter's Dog* (The Sportsman's Press) are as applicable now as then:

'The understanding between a good working pointer-retriever and his trainer is not achieved in a few weeks, or even months, indeed it often takes years to achieve and many people achieve it only once in a lifetime, if at all. It should be the aim of all who own a pointer-retriever to achieve this harmony between dog and man, or something close to it. This book is intended to provide a guide towards that goal. It can be nothing more than a guide, since dog and man should be learning from each other throughout their respective lifetimes and each combination is different, but at least it should serve to help the novice who otherwise does not know where to begin.'

My thanks are due to: K. H. Grose, Ian Glass and my wife Evelyn for the thankless task of reading and commenting on the typescript, but for any opinions, mistakes or omissions, I am entirely responsible.

Introduction

This is a book about training the pointer-retriever, a hunting dog which should be able to range wide, or close, according to the nature of the ground and the instructions it receives from its handler. It should be able to find game and, when found, should indicate the whereabouts by coming on point and holding that point steadily until the handler arrives within range and the order is given to flush. Once flushed and shot the dog should be able to retrieve the dead, or wounded, game to hand. It should, ideally, be able to work with equal facility in the open, in cover and in water. Since such a dog must be a combination of pointer, working chiefly on air scents, and retriever, working mostly on ground scents, and its range must vary as indicated, it can only be described as a variable-range, variable-pace, pointer-retriever.

If this might seem to be expecting too much from one dog it should be appreciated that for years the slow and steady, or swift and darting, short-range pointer-retriever has been with us in the shape of the spaniel in its various forms, from the Clumber to the Springer. In the early 19th century, prior to the development of the double-barrelled breech-loading shotgun, all retrievers were expected to hold game, if not point, and all pointers, or setters, were expected to retrieve. The following description of a shooting dog is taken from *The Sporting Magazine* of 1832:

'A Pointer or Setter to deserve the name should hunt high but steadily; quarter his ground with truth and judgement; turn to hand or whistle; drop to hand, bird and shot; back at all distances; be steady from a hare, yet follow a wounded one if necessary; and recover a dead or wounded bird well.'

This is a good description of the behaviour expected of the pointer-retriever breeds today. The spaniel then, as now, was expected to work within shot, hunting out his game and bustling it up within range of the muzzle-loading guns. The retriever breeds, in so far as they were as yet established, were either expected to work as a spaniel within range of the gun, or, if working further afield, to point, or set, the game in the manner of the pointer-retriever breeds of today. They were all then acknowledged to be hunting dogs and it is thus that they are still widely regarded throughout the greater part of the world. Only in Britain where an artificial distinction between hunting and shooting developed during the 18th and 19th centuries are they merely termed ambiguously gundogs, although even here the pointer-retriever breeds are classified by the Kennel Club as those which 'hunt, point and retrieve.'

During the first half of the 19th century in most of Europe, apart from France where the revolution had already partly abolished class distinctions, shooting was strictly the sport of the nobility and the emergent middle classes and peasants were not allowed to own hunting dogs. In these circumstances it is understandable that 'battue' shooting, the term then used for driven game shooting, when the birds were driven by beaters over the waiting guns, was common in Europe, although at that time frowned on by British sportsmen as slaughter fit only for foreigners. Such sporting dogs as then existed in the greater part of Europe were the property of the nobility.

With the revolutions of the late 1840s the face of Europe was abruptly changed. The old decadent aristocracy were overthrown and killed, or banished. As in France, their estates became public property. From this stage onwards the emergent middle classes were able to own dogs and take an interest in shooting. Their aim was to find suitable breeds of pointer-retrievers to find the now much scarcer game, rather than attempt to emulate the driven shooting of the vanished nobility in their erstwhile strictly preserved estates.

It was not only in Europe that things altered abruptly during the latter half of the 19th century. Although the Victorian age is often represented as one of little change in outlook and of permanently fixed ideas, this is far from the truth. There was a complete turn around in the sporting scene in Britain from the 1850s onwards. Whereas in the 1830s, as indicated by the above quotation, shooting was largely over dogs and driven game, or 'battue', shooting was widely considered more like slaughter than sport, three factors brought about a major change in sporting thought in the latter half of the 19th century. The first was the invention of the double-barrelled breech-loading shotgun. The second was the farming slump of the 1860s and '70s, caused initially by the influx of cheap grain from the mid-West states of the U.S.A. followed by the importation of frozen meat from the Argentine and Australia. The third was the drastic revision of the complex old Game Laws, which had taken place in the 1850s, making it much simpler to obtain a licence to shoot game.

The ease of shooting with a double-barrelled breech-loading shotgun and the fact that farms in Britain were actually worth more to rent as shoots than for crops, or cattle, combined with intensive game rearing, as well as the revision of the complex old Game Laws, which enabled the emergent professional middle classes to take to the sport in droves, inevitably led to a vast increase in driven shooting. Shooting over dogs quickly went out of fashion. With the foundation of the Kennel Club in 1873 two categories of gundog were soon recognised, firstly retrievers and secondly pointers and setters. It was not until the turn of the century that the spaniel was recognised and not until the 1970s that the pointer-retriever was at last accepted under the equivocal 'hunt, point and retrieve' category, bringing the wheel full circle once more.

In Germany during the latter half of the 19th century the Gordon Setter was popular as a useful pointer-retriever, capable of finding game and retrieving it. The Germans, however, with typical Teutonic thoroughness, decided to breed a dog specifically as a pointer-retriever. The first records of the dog which came to be known as the Kurzhaar, or, as it is known in Britain, the German Shorthaired Pointer, date from the early 1870s. By the end of the decade it had become established and the records from then onwards show a gradually improving type of dog, resulting from a mixture of crosses of indigenous breeds, notably the old Hanoverian Schweisshund, and probably some English pointer blood.

Other pointer-retriever breeds, of course, were also emerging during the same period. The Weimaraner, supposedly descended from dogs bred by the Counts of Weimar, and the Magyar Vizsla, or Hungarian Pointer, descended from dogs used by the old Hungarian aristocracy were only two of the more prominent. The Pudel-Pointer, descended from a poodle-pointer cross established in the 1890s, the Munsterlanders and Wirehaired pointers and others such as the wirehaired pointing Griffon and the Brittany Spaniel all appear to have developed during much the same period.

The truth is that any dog worked in front of the gun as a gamefinder, soon learns to distinguish between air and foot scents. The pointer, or setter, roading out the scent of a covey of grouse that have been flushed is clearly seen to be working on foot scent, after initially having found the covey and come on point on air scent. When the retriever trained to work within gunshot catches an air scent its tail starts to move and it begins to advance showing interest. Its owner should have had sufficient warning to be ready as the game is flushed. With just a little training such a dog could easily enough be taught to point. Almost any breed of gundog could be taught to work in the way that was common to them all a matter of a hundred and fifty years ago, quartering the ground, finding game, pointing it and then retrieving it once shot. Training and experience are the most important factors.

There is not a great deal of difference between the pointer, or setter, working to hand signals and whistle, quartering the ground in front of its handler, and the well trained retriever working far out in front of its handler in response to signal and whistle. It is the ability to work at a distance in harmony with its handler that always seems so outstanding to the spectator. In many ways it is easier to achieve this with a natural pointer-retriever than it is with a specialist retriever breed, since the former should point when coming on game at a distance, whereas to the latter this is often merely a temptation to chase.

The fact of the matter is that most people are afraid to let their dog range beyond gunshot, simply because they have seen dogs run wild and flush game out of shot. It is in this aspect of training the pointer-retriever that most people, at least initially, go wrong. It is important to let the pointer-retriever roam freely, but equally it is important to attain a high degree of initial obedience, even where the youngster shows a natural instinct to point from an early age. Paradoxically it is often because a dog shows great instinct initially that the owner fails to train it properly. There is a certain fatal familiarity about the words:

'He started pointing and retrieving, so I just took him out with the gun and he worked perfectly.'

Just as beauty is in the eye of the beholder so any degree of perfection attained by such a dog is usually only in the eye of its owner. It is easy to forget a generally deplorable standard in the thrill of one or two pleasing points, or retrieves. Yet with a little perseverance in training many disappointments or mistakes could probably have been avoided and a much higher standard attained, especially with any dog that has a deeply ingrained instinct. It is always a recipe for disaster to leave everything to the dog, however natural a worker it may be.

Naturally, not all dogs will achieve the same standards, however well they may be trained. There are always some that have a far greater capacity for work and far more deeply ingrained instinct that others. Then again some handlers will expect more from their dogs than others and some will be satisfied with less, failing to get the best from their dog. Inevitably there will be considerable differences between dogs themselves, even in the same litter. Some may be naturally fast and wide ranging, others may be naturally slower and tending to range closer. One dog will always stand absolutely staunch on point from its very first sight point as a puppy, while another will always wave its tail very slightly. One dog will be a natural retriever, picking up and carrying from an early age, another will take endless training before finally retrieving to hand. It does not always follow that the one will be better than the other. An enormous amount must depend on the trainer, the dog, its breeding, the amount of work it has and the variety of that work.

It stands to reason that the dog which is, for instance, only worked on a moor will find itself at something of a loss when it is first introduced to pheasants on low ground. In the same way a dog which has never seen grouse, or worked on a moor, but has only worked in small fields in one of the southern counties of England will naturally be at a loss when faced with the daunting expanse of a heather covered hill in Sutherland. Neither would feel at home when taken on a foreshore for an evening's flighting for the first time. No pointer-retriever can be expected to master all aspects of the very varied work it may be expected to cover without considerable training and experience in the field, however good a natural worker it may be either as a pointer, or as a retriever.

Of course a very great deal must depend on what the trainer expects from the dog. Some people will have shooting which requires far more retrieving than pointing. Others may require the dog to find game in sparsely populated acres and quartering and pointing will be most important. Yet others will have ground with a great deal of cover, and yet others will require a particularly good water dog. The pointer-retriever should fulfill all these roles, but it clearly cannot be expected to learn everything that is required in one season.

It is always important in any event with all pointer-retrievers to provide plenty of variety, both in training and in work. If, for instance, the youngster is too often forced to walk at heel in training, it may later become difficult to get it to quarter freely when required to do so. Equally, to take another obvious example, if the dog is always allowed to roam freely it will clearly become difficult to get it to remain at heel when required. Too much of any one form of work when training is undesirable since it is likely to inhibit other aspects of work and curb the dog's all-round ability.

From the complete novice's viewpoint the most important thing is to have a clear overall picture of how to train the youngster to become a pointer-retriever. Not only is it desirable to know the steps by which the dog may be trained and, if possible, the likely resistances to training which may be encountered, but it is also essential to know exactly what it is hoped to achieve as a result of the training. Unless the novice trainer has at the back of his, or her, mind a clear picture of the aims of the training, including not only what the young dog is expected to learn, but also at least roughly how it is to be achieved, the end results are hardly likely to be successful.

The chief problem facing the novice is that no set time-tables can be provided and no specific answers can be given to any particular situation. Suggestions may be made and may be acted on successfully, or alternatively they may fail. Nothing about training animals is ever certain of success. All that can be done is to indicate various likely methods of training the pointer-retriever and the likely resistances which may be encountered. It is up to the handler to try to achieve initially at least some understanding with the dog and once a degree of communication has been achieved to go on from there.

No rules of training are infallible. Indeed rules of training are in themselves somewhat suspect. The trainer should always have an open mind, prepared to react to the dog as each situation demands. Above all, however, the trainer should not allow any situation to arise where a confrontation becomes inevitable. Before any such situation arises it is highly desirable to halt the lesson and return to it on another occasion when both dog and trainer are fresh. It is also desirable to start again in such circumstances that any mistakes made previously will not be allowed to recur. The trainer, after all, should be able to think ahead and it is up to him, or her, to use this ability to good advantage.

Whether the trainer feels the dog should start pointing first, or retrieving first must be a question for each individual dog and trainer to decide. There are those who advocate no retrieving in the first season in case the dog does not remain staunch on point. There are others who maintain that retrieving should be taught before pointing. While it is true that initially pointing and retrieving should be kept quite separate, at least in the dog's mind, it is probably never wise to stifle instinct when it begins to assert itself. It may even be necessary to channel the instincts to point and to retrieve at the same time, but separately. Each case should be assessed on its own merits.

With any young dog the important thing is never to overdo the training. A bored dog will react in a number of ways, from deliberate disobedience to sulleness. It is better by far to keep each lesson short and full of variety than to keep on repeating one aspect of the training. With a young dog, especially, the lessons should be kept as light hearted as possible and the dog should always be praised whenever it does the right thing. Such points will be made further on, but they cannot be emphasised too often.

Almost certainly much of what I write will be regarded as old stuff by many readers, but there may be some who are new to the idea of pointer-retrievers, or for that matter to training any hunting dog. It is primarily for them that this book is intended, although many owners of pointer-retrievers may find it useful to have their ideas put into concrete form and some of the suggestions put forward may be new to them. The important point, which I trust will be fully driven home, is that to train a pointer-retriever well can easily last a dog's lifetime, with both trainer and dog constantly learning from each other. It is certainly necessary to take a good deal of time and trouble over it in order to achieve success. If a season's sport is curtailed and some shooting days missed that might otherwise have been had, that is a small price to pay. It should be worth it many times over in the satisfaction that is finally to be had from watching the dog that you have trained quarter the ground, find the game, point it staunchly, flush it to command and then retrieve it to hand. Then indeed it will all seem worth while.

1 Initial Decisions

Although this is primarily a book about training that group of gundogs classified by the Kennel Club in Britain as being 'German Shorthaired Pointers and those breeds which hunt, point and retrieve', it should be appreciated that less than a hundred and fifty years ago almost all gundogs were expected to work in this way. I have seen Labradors even today trained in this fashion which worked extremely well as Pointer-Retrievers. Wide ranging large Springers have always worked very much in this way and before it became fashionable for Pointers and Setters to specialise in pointing only they were often excellent retrievers. The Gordon Setter was regarded in Germany in the late 19th century as the perfect all-round Pointer-Retriever. Simply because Victorian and Edwardian fashion decreed that retrievers and pointers should become specialist dogs does not mean to say that they cannot still be perfectly well trained on the lines indicated in this book, if their owner so wishes.

Today the Kennel Club in Britain recognises four classifications of gundog. The first is Retrievers, which covers Black, or Yellow, Labradors, Chesapeakes, Curly, or Flat, Coated Retrievers and Golden Retrievers. In the second classification are Pointers and Setters, covering English Pointers and English, Gordon and Irish Setters. The third classification is Spaniels, covering Clumbers, Cockers, English and Welsh Springers, Sussex, and finally Irish Water Spaniels. The fourth classification is German Shorthaired Pointers and those breeds which hunt, point and retrieve. This covers German Shorthaired Pointers, Weimaraners, Magyar Vizslas, also known as Hungarian Pointers, Large Munsterlanders and Wirehaired Pointers.

Originally the German Shorthaired Pointer, the Weimaraner and the Magyar Vizsla were the only breeds recognised in the fourth category. The Large Munsterlander and German Wirehaired Pointer were subsequent additions and are steadily establishing themselves. If sufficient numbers of any other Pointer-Retriever breeds, such as the Small Munsterlander, or the Pudel-Pointer, were to be registered with the Kennel Club and a breed society formed and approved by the Kennel Club they would then automatically be included in the fourth classification.

The Kennel Club's role viz-a-viz dogs is very similar to that of the Jockey Club in the world of thoroughbred horse racing. It is, however, a good deal more powerful in its own way. Every breed society, indeed every field trial and show society, has to be registered with the Kennel Club as an affiliated society. Each breed's standard has to be registered with the Kennel Club, as do all field trial and show judges. All field trials and shows must be run under the rules laid down by the Kennel Club. Every pedigree dog must be registered with the Kennel Club and each litter of pups by pedigree parents must also be registered at birth. Each prize won in field trial or show must be recorded. Within the sphere of pedigree dogs the Kennel Club is all-powerful.

The Kennel Club and the affiliated breed clubs are not, of course, concerned with anything but pedigree dogs. Cross-breeds, or mongrels of any kind, cannot be registered with the Kennel Club, although sometimes excellent working dogs. They cannot therefore enter field trials or shows run under Kennel Club jurisdiction. A more basic reason why it is not desirable to buy a cross-bred dog, or any sort of mongrel, however good looking, or however good a worker, is simply that it is unlikely to breed progeny like itself, either in looks, or working ability. Second generations of cross-bred dogs seldom breed true to sire or dam, and are generally not as good workers. The novice would do well to avoid any such crosses and stick to pedigree stock.

While the Kennel Club is the ultimate authority on all matters concerning pedigree dogs it must be seen to be impartial at all times. The Kennel Club therefore cannot, indeed must not, advise enquiring novices as to which breeds to choose. It is quite outside their function to do more than indicate the various breeds within the four categories of gundog and their breed standards. If approached, however, the Secretary of the Kennel Club will happily provide a list of breed clubs, with the secretaries' names and addresses. It is then up to the enquirer to carry out his own investigations as to which breed of gundog will suit him best.

The secretaries of the breed societies will usually be happy to help any enquirer and will advise on their breed and provide the names of individual members with breeding kennels. They will also, if asked, provide the dates, times and whereabouts of field trials, shows and working tests for the breed. They will almost certainly be extremely helpful and ready to answer any questions about their breed. It is advisable, however, to bear in mind that unlike the Kennel Club they have no duty to remain impartial.

On the whole, however, breed societies are fairly sensible about warning the novice of the requirements of their breed of gundog. Similarly reputable breeders prefer to find good homes for their pups and will generally warn prospective buyers if they feel they are not fully aware of what to expect. If a prospective home is clearly unsuitable they will usually prefer to forego a sale in such circumstances. It is not, however, advisable to rely on such forebearance. There are always those less reputable kennels only too eager to make a sale regardless. On the other hand after a few visits even the greenest novice will probably appreciate the difference between the two kinds of breeder. He, or she, will also have begun to see how the various dogs compare with each other and will have begun to get a clearer picture of the breed in his, or her, mind.

Undoubtedly, the best thing that any interested enquirer can do in the first instance, however, is to visit the field trials, shows and working tests, the details of which were obtained from the breed club secretaries. Here on view is a broad cross section of the various breeds, demonstrating their working abilities and their breed standards. There will also be numerous enthusiastic owners and from their comments it will very soon be possible to form a clearer picture.

Even if the enquiring novice has no interest in shows and only wants a working dog it will still be worth attending one or two, for sometimes a quite different type of dog is to be found there as opposed to field trials, or working tests. It will very soon become obvious in which breeds there is a deep cleavage between show types and working types and which blood lines are amongst the more notable in each sphere. Ideally it is desirable to aim for a blood line which can take prizes in the show ring and in field trials for this indicates both inherent good looks and sound working ability.

Apart from assessing the various breeds' working abilities and appearance on such occasions, undoubtedly the greatest benefit the novice will gain is the opportunity to talk to ordinary dog owners and discuss the points they find in favour of their breed over the others. Such ordinary owners are also likely to discuss far more frankly than prominent breeders the disadvantages of their breed. Remember, however, that on the whole they must be en-thusiasts or they would not be there in the first place. The impor-tant thing above all at this stage is to avoid becoming committed to any one breed, or perhaps, more importantly, any one pup, before having gained an overall picture of the various breeds and decided which is most suitable for you.

Although most of the foregoing would seem fairly obvious common sense it never ceases to surprise me how many appar-ently otherwise sensible people will approach the question of choosing their first gundog with rather less thought than, for instance, buying a tin of beans at their local supermarket. Buy-ing a gundog puppy is often very little more than a similar type of impulse buy, although frequently inspired initially by the syn-drome known as 'keeping up with the Jones's'. A gundog of a cer-tain breed, especially one of the less common Pointer-Retriever varieties, is observed, either working well, or just looking attrac-tive, and the decision is half-made. The sight of a litter for sale short-ly afterwards and the deed is done, all too often to be regretted later at leisure.

If as little thought were to be applied to the care and training of the dog then the new owners would do well not to have bought it in the first place. This, sadly, is certainly true of a minority of owners once the novelty has finally worn off and they realise that they now own an animal requiring regular exercise and work, as well as attention. The dog will then most probably be advertised in some local paper, destined to be given away to the first home that is offered, the second step on a downward path usually leading to a sad end.

In such cases, where it is lucky, the wretched animal may first be offered back to the kennels where it was bred. If they have room and it has not yet been ruined by careless handling past the point of no return, it is likely to be accepted, especially where they value their stock and their reputation sufficiently, for obviously this type of owner is bound to be nothing but a bad advertisment. A reputable breeder will always try to avoid selling to unsuitable owners of this kind, but unfortunately they are not always easy to recognise in advance.

Anyone who has ever bred gundogs seriously will know the kind of person who seems to all intents and purposes a sound prospective owner, only to prove a complete disappointment. Typical was the case of the doctor who was once warmly recommended to me as a keen shooting man likely to provide a good working home for a dog. He came to me shortly afterwards when I had a litter available and seemed a pleasant, sensible person. He had kept gundogs before and apparently knew what he was about, even if he had not had one of that particular breed. He lived on the outskirts of a city, but close to wide open spaces where he could exercise his dog each day. He seemed in every way perfect, but soon after he had bought the pup he began to make complaints and it was not long before I realised I had made a bad mistake both from the pup's viewpoint and my own. The only solution in the end was to take the dog back for its sake and mine.

Yet, generally, once a puppy has been bought, a conscious pride in ownership asserts itself. Quite often thereafter the person who so innocently embarked on dog ownership becomes an enthusiast. He, or she, joins breed clubs and training classes, then enters shows, working tests and field trials, but, sadly, quite often to little avail because that first choice, so carelessly entered into, was what in the motor trade is descriptively termed 'a lemon'. They may have literally been sold a useless pup and however much they may strive to improve it there is virtually nothing to be done but to get rid of it to a good home and start again. This is not an easy decision to take since it amounts to an admission of failure, but it is better to do so than to waste endless time and energy attempting to transform a toad into a prince, or princess. That is a feat seldom performed outside fairy tales.

Unfortunately there must be many who, had they started with a puppy more worthy of their time and energy, could have become the owners of a field trial champion. Beware then of rushing into buying a puppy of the first gundog breed that attracts the eye. It cannot be stressed too strongly that to judge any breed of gundog on a few individuals is shortsighted in the extreme. Those seen may have been outstanding and quite unrepresentative, or, more probably, they are likely to have been mediocre specimens, not truly representative of the better qualities of the breed.

When buying a puppy it must surely be obvious that it is worth taking time and trouble to ensure that you are obtaining a specimen which is capable of developing into a first rate example of the breed, both as regards looks and working ability. In the best instances the two should go together. As a first step it is desirable to consider carefully the characteristics, the temperament, looks and working abilities of the sire and dam and if possible check back on their breeding before worrying about the pups. By carefully studying their background it is possible to know in advance whether the pups are likely to be worth consideration. Good pups are merely a reflection of sound breeding, they do not generally appear from haphazard matings.

Although it is often difficult to appreciate the fact when looking at a litter of two month old puppies the physical, and to some extent mental, characteristics which are going to be present in the adult dog are already visible. The presence, or absence, of bone, the free movements of a well formed dog, the shape of the head and the formation of the jaws are as they will be when the pup is a grown dog, even though not always easy to visualise. That is certainly the best time to judge a pup against the rest of the litter.

Much harder to judge is the pup of some four or five months upwards to eighteen months or more. Then the gawkiness of uneven adolescent growth can easily make a promising pup seem less desirable, or a premature maturity may conceal the fact that a pup will grow into an overmuscled, unbalanced dog. In addition by then various unfavourable resistances to training may have developed through careless handling, or by pure accident, but in either case making future training a more difficult process than it should have been. In general it is preferable to choose a pup prior to weaning and remove it to its new home as soon as it has been properly weaned at around eight or ten weeks.

It is advisable to remember that choosing a pup is a long term decision in that all being well the pup of your choice is likely to be with you as a gundog and companion, not to mention friend, for anything up to a decade or more. It is easy to feel when you make the purchase that if you decide later you have made a mistake you can simply get rid of it. By the time that stage has been reached, and passed, you may well find that you have grown too fond of the animal and despite its obvious faults, which, reluctantly, by then, you have come to appreciate all too well, you would prefer to keep it rather than part with it. Be warned that it is easy to make this mistake.

If you are married it is also perhaps just as well to bear in mind that on occasions gundogs have been the cause of divorces, and, where a marriage has ended in divorce anyway, the gundog has often been a bitter bone of contention. Even the best of gundogs can unwittingly be the cause of marital strife for one reason or another, be it only because of such matters as mud on the best carpet, or some other social indiscretion on the part of the gundog or handler. It is desirable therefore to consider the spouse when buying a gundog pup. Some breeds are good family dogs and some are not so good, although in general most gundogs can be relied on to adapt readily enough to family life. Divorce, however, is liable to have a disruptive and unsettling effect on any gundog's training and should in general be avoided, wherever possible, at least until the dog is fully trained!

At this stage it is advisable to bear in mind the proposed breed and to consider the differences between a long haired and a short-haired dog. However much one may admire long haired dogs they are bound to become muddy and tangled with burrs after a day's shooting. Apart from the dirt, this entails a good deal of extra work keeping the dog's coat clean and with the best will in the world when they are moulting in the spring, hairs will get everywhere. To be fair the shorthaired coats are almost as bad in this latter respect, but they are easier to clean after a day's shooting. They certainly do not require such extensive grooming and nor do they cause quite as much dirt around the house, or car.

It has also to be admitted that some breeds of gundogs are clearly better around the house than others. Equally some gundogs are probably better in kennels than others, although both these may be regarded as individual traits rather than as breed characteristics. In the same way some are naturally clean and others are naturally dirty. On the other hand some breeds of gundog certainly require considerable exercise and attention, whereas others require less. A great deal must depend on individuals in every breed, but these are all points which should be borne in mind when selecting a pup, for in such respects they will probably take after their sire or dam. There is certainly no harm in asking about such points, but, of course, the answers may not always be strictly accurate.

Before buying any breed of gundog the would-be owner should also first reflect on his, or her, own circumstances. It is all very well being sure in your own mind which breed you prefer, but that is not necessarily the same as the breed which is most suitable for you. The two may not always be the same and it may be necessary to compromise, for there is no point in buying a breed that for one reason or another is totally unsuitable. This is a factor which is far too often not even considered beforehand, let alone weighed in the balance. The concept of a Great Dane in the top floor of a high rise block of flats is no more absurd, or unfortunate, than a Pointer-Retriever breed in a city house, or flat, with no garden for exercise, condemned to walk the streets on a lead without hope of escape from the exhaust fumes of passing traffic and only the relief of occasional 'romps' in an overpopulated park, never indulging in the work which allows his instincts their proper outlet and fulfilment.

Unless the prospective gundog owner can ensure that his, or her, dog will have opportunities available to work in the manner for which it was bred, he, or she, should have very serious misgivings about owning such an animal. Whereas the prospective owner can sublimate his, or her, desire to own a gundog by acquiring a dog of some similar, but non-working, breed, the dog itself can never fully sublimate its natural desire to work in the manner for which its ancestors have been bred for generations. This can lead to moroseness and sullen behaviour, or plain refusal to obey orders, or to vices such as fighting with other dogs, or, given the chance, sheep worrying. It is not the fault of the dog. It is the fault of the owner, who refused to recognise that his circumstances were such that he should never have acquired any gundog breed. This is more especially the case with any of the Pointer-Retriever breeds.

It is unfortunately all too common for someone to buy a gundog and either refuse, or be unable, to allow it free rein for its natural instincts. While keeping it only as a pet, or only entering it in shows, thus refusing its natural instincts a chance to develop, such a dog may well seem perfectly happy and normal throughout its life. It has, however, been stultified, repressed and unnaturally restrained. In such circumstances the reaction is often quite violent, although not necessarily in the first generation. Gunshyness, hysteria, general nervousness, chewing, whining, endless, mindless barking, even fits of savage behaviour, attacking other dogs, or humans, without warning, are all symptoms not uncommon in dogs thus deprived of a natural outlet for their instincts. Yet when one considers the matter any gundog kept in a city is automatically being deprived of its natural existence.

If it seems at first sight a sweeping assertion to say that it is wrong to keep gundogs in a city environment this is, of course, subject to exceptions. Where a suitable area such as a large garden and a nearby common, or parkland, is available this may, given occasional visits to the country, be enough. If a country home is also regularly visited then it may be that a city-bound gundog will still have a reasonable existence. The important point is that any gundog should have the opportunity for regular exercise in suitable surroundings where his instincts can be properly fulfilled.

It is simply not enough, even in the country, just to open the door each day and turn the dog loose, imagining that he will exercise himself, although this is unhappily all too often the practice in many housing estates around the country. This is the sort of thing that results in a gundog learning all sorts of bad habits, usually ending up by being run over, or by chasing sheep, or similar vices. It was thus, I ultimately discovered, that the doctor, mentioned earlier, thought it proper to exercise the pup he had bought from me with, in due course, inevitable results.

Quite apart from exercise it is highly desirable, wherever any gundog lives, to let him have some shooting experience if at all possible. If the gundog owner has no shoot of his, or her, own on which to exercise the dog there are still possible substitutes. He, or she, may well be able to train the pup to the stage where it can enter working tests and acquit itself creditably, from that he, or she, may even move on to field trials. It may well thus be possible to train the dog to the point where it will be readily accepted for picking up at local shoots if those are available. It is not even necessary for the owner himself to shoot, for by asking the local keepers, or shooting syndicates, it may be possible to get permission to act as a beater with the dog, as long as it is up to a reasonable standard. Any such opportunities to let a gundog exercise its natural instincts, however, should be organised in advance before obtaining a pup rather than sought after the event. It is highly desirable to know in advance that the pup will have a sound outlet for his instincts, rather than thinking of this after the purchase.

In this respect it is advisable to think doubly hard before buying any of the pointer-retriever breeds. Any owner of these breeds which have been bred to hunt, point and retrieve is likely to find opportunities for fulfilment of each aspect of the dog's working role difficult to obtain. Quite simply the roughshooting country where such a dog is most at home is not today readily available as more and more of our countryside is swallowed up by concrete each year. It is very tempting to exercise such a gundog simply as a retriever, or less commonly simply as a pointer, rather than in his full role. In either function the dog may perform very well indeed, but in neither alone is it fulfilling the purpose for which it was bred.

A dog of any of the pointer-retriever breeds really requires varied ground to work over and plenty of opportunities to do so. It should be able to work in water, in cover and in the open with equal facility. It should be able to work its ground, hunting at speed, and come on point instantly on fur or feather. It should drop to flush and shot, and mark the fall of game. It should then be able to follow a runner and retrieve from water, or cover, and bring the quarry to hand. In order to perform these varied functions it requires varied ground and varied quarries. Ideally a large stretch of marginal land with moor on the upper stretches and bog and riverside plantations on the low ground would be perfect. Few people are fortunate enough, however, to possess such excellent facilities.

Simply to work a moor pointing the game, or sitting at heel at a driven shoot, retrieving after each drive, is not enough for one of these gundog breeds. Let the prospective owner, who requires a specialist dog such as a retriever, or a pointer, or a spaniel, choose such a breed and do his, or her, best to ensure that its instinct is properly fulfilled. To take one of the pointer-retriever breeds and use it only as a retriever, a pointer, or a spaniel, is totally wrong, although by no means uncommon. It would be far better to consider training a retriever, or a setter, on pointer-retriever lines. The dog would at least then find its instincts being fully stretched and would probably respond excellently to the challenge.

Assuming, however, that the prospective owner has selected the right breed and has sufficient opportunities to train and work his, or her, chosen pup in suitable surroundings, it is still important that he, or she, has everything prepared for its arrival. It is surprising how many owners cannot make up their minds prior the arrival of their pup whether it is to be kept in the house or in a kennel. In either case it is, of course, important to have everything prepared beforehand.

When the pup is to be kept in a kennel this should be roomy, but well lit and well ventilated. If it is brick, or stone, built it should have a raised wooden bed clear of draughts. It is desirable to have a good concrete run outside, preferably totally enclosed in stout chain link fencing embedded in concrete. In the run there should be a stout wooden bench providing both shade and a resting place off the concrete when required. There should also be a ready supply of water, with, or without, an automatic drinking bowl.

If possible it should be south facing and adjacent to the house. It should not, above all, be in a totally walled off area, where the dog can neither see, nor hear, anything that is happening. This can lead to boredom and vices, also to nervousness. Next to the concrete run itself it is highly desirable to have a well fenced grass run, but this is not necessary if the dog is to be kept in the house during the day and only kennelled at night. What type of bedding is used, whether straw, sawdust, or shredded paper is a matter of individual preference and to some extent availability.

It is undesirable to keep a gundog for too long in a centrally heated house since this can clearly lower its natural resistance to cold. Where the dog is to be kept in the house it is important that from the first it should have a special sleeping place of its own. Somewhere such as the bottom of a cupboard with a raised padded bed is ideal, providing a quiet place of its own out of the light and general noise. In each room to which it has access the dog should also have a corner which it may regard as its special place to which it can and should retire. There is nothing worse than an unruly gundog in a house leaping onto chairs, upsetting small tables, or sweeping glasses and other breakables onto the floor with its frantically waving tail.

A gundog introduced into the house in this way will soon become accustomed to the house routine and adapt to it perfectly well. Inevitably, of course, there are both advantages and disadvantages in keeping a gundog, or gundogs, in the house. However personally clean the dog itself may be, there is bound to be a certain amount of extra dirt caused. In addition the dog will require a regular water supply, to which it should have access when it wishes.

The all important feature of keeping a gundog in the house, even for only a part of the day, is ensuring that everyone in the household, who may have contact with it, understands the training programme. Unless this is the case it is almost always better to keep the dog in the kennel for the greater part of the day. Where a dog is taught one set of standards out shooting, or in training sessions, and another in the house it is too much to expect good results. This is especially so where there are children playing with a dog, when bad habits can so very readily be inculcated which are hard, if not impossible, to eradicate.

If different commands are used in the house from those used

when out shooting, or during training, then clearly the dog is going to be confused to say the least. It is essential therefore to make sure that the dog receives similar commands at home and when outside. Orders in the house should be kept to the minimum, but should also be enforced every bit as much as in the field, for once slackness sets in the dog will be quick to take advantage of it. It is therefore very important where the dog is to be in the house to ensure that the entire household all know what commands to use and stick to them only, as well as strictly enforcing them when they are used. This is, unfortunately, seldom entirely the case to put it mildly, but a dog which lives even part time in the house probably still gains something over the dog kept solely in the kennel.

Once all these points have been decided and the pup has finally been chosen and has been satisfactorily weaned it is advisable to collect it as soon as possible so that you may start its acclimatisation and initial training at once. It is, of course, infinitely preferable to go the kennels and pick up your chosen pup yourself, rather than have it sent to you by any other means of transport. Apart from anything else this is a good opportunity to have a final check with the breeder regarding any points which may have been overlooked. In most cases this is likely to save a great deal of telephoning and correspondence.

For instance it is essential to know whether the pup has had its initial Epivax and other injections against disease, which are so vitally important. It may well be that the pup has had only the first of these, in which case it is important to collect the necessary certificates for your own vet to complete the course. If it has not had any as yet it cannot be stressed too strongly how important it is to ensure that there is no chance of the pup picking up any infection before it has been injected. It has only to sniff the urine of an infected dog to pick up canine hepatitis, or leptospirosis, both of which are usually fatal.

It is also desirable to know the various feeding times to which the pup has been accustomed, since, however inconvenient these may be, it is better at least at the start to continue with them for a while. While on the subject it is as well to check on the diet to which the pup is accustomed and continue to feed it as far as possible with the same type of meal and biscuit to avoid initial upsets. This is also a suitable time to pick up the pedigree and Kennel Club Certificates, as well as signing the transfer certificate, which requires both breeder's and owner's signature. This can then be sent direct to the Kennel Club saving both parties unnecessary correspondence.

If the pup is being transported in a travelling kennel in the back of an estate wagon, Land Rover, or car, it is a good plan to take some of its bedding and mix it with whatever you have provided so that it will feel itself in familiar rather than strange surroundings. If the pup is travelling on someone's knee, or beside someone in the car, it is advisable to rub a blanket over the dam and over the pup itself, then offer it this to lie on, so that once again it smells familiar scents round it. In either case it is a good plan to give it something to chew, such as a marrow bone, or some plaything, to keep it occupied on the journey. If it is not inside a kennel it is also advisable to have plenty of newspaper on hand in case it is sick while travelling.

There are, of course, occasions when the pup cannot be fetched personally, but, having had experience of sending pups by plane, train, boat and road, I can only say that by all these varied means of transport there is always the chance of it being handled carelessly by some insensitive idiot. That this is due to nothing more than thoughtlessness, or even accident, makes it no better. While very often it may only cause a temporary setback it can also have very long lasting effects, even resulting in permanent damage in the case of a sensitive pup.

By its very nature the best and stoutest of travelling kennels provides limited visibility and space. Even where the breeder has sensibly done his, or her, best to accustom the pup to it beforehand, merely to be locked inside such a limited space must be a traumatic experience for a sensitive youngster suddenly removed from its familiar surroundings. It only requires, for example, a jet engine to start up as a pup is being carried past in its kennel to give even the toughest and most phlegmatic of pups a very considerable fright, which can affect it for a long time.

If the pup has to travel by one or other of the means of transport mentioned, the vendor should provide it with a good sized returnable travelling kennel, with plenty of bedding, clearly labelled for its destination with the addresses and telephone numbers of both sender and consignee. If the journey is likely to be a long one food should also be provided, with instructions regarding feeding and watering as and when required. It is normally best if, prior to its departure, the pup can be fed a tranquilliser prescribed by the vet as this will help to keep it sleepy throughout the journey and thus less likely to be adversely affected by the noise and handling.

In addition to supplies of food and bowls for both food and water securely fixed inside the travelling kennel, the pup should also be provided with a collar and a stout chain. If travelling by British Rail their regulations also insist on a muzzle being provided, although it need not be worn, if the pup is confined at all times. All this may sound unnecessary, but a strike of airport, shipping, railway, or transport staff, fog, blizzards or accidents may all result in delays which cannot be anticipated. While in such cases due care is almost always paid to animals caught in transit it is best to be prepared for the worst and ensure that the pup is at least well supplied for every possible contingency.

Prior to the pup's reception it should have been decided by what name it is to be known about the house, as distinct from the name by which it is registered at the Kennel Club. Double barrelled names such as Hamlet of Haycock may be all very well for registration purposes, but they are clearly undesirable for training. Hamlet, or even Haycock, by themselves might just be acceptable, but more grandiose names, such as Emperor Moonshine of Brocklebank, obviously cannot be contemplated for everyday use. All training should be conducted on a sensible basis and everything, including the commands, should be kept as short as possible. The same goes for the pup's name.

Some thought and care should be given to selecting a good short name for the pup. Initially it will be used to attract the pup's attention to commands. The best canine names, therefore, are short and monosyllabic, easily repeated and easily heard. Names such as Sam, Kate, Dan, Pat and so on are all good names for a pup. It is desirable, however, to avoid names such as Teal, which closely resembles 'Heel', or Kit, which resembles 'Sit'. Anything which might cause confusion in the pup's mind is clearly best avoided. In this particular case care should also be taken not to choose a name belonging to anyone in, or closely associated with, the family since this can lead on occasions not only to confusion, but also to embarrassment, as for instance when the name is shouted in public with uncomplimentary epithets attached.

Throughout the pup's training there should be no need for expensive and elaborate equipment such as dummy launchers, or electronic dog collars. The former may be used in the later stages of the training, if the trainer feels it would be useful, but initially it can have disadvantages and if an assistant can be obtained that is always preferable. An electronic dog collar is an even more expensive item and requires using with considerable care. They are not advisable for novice trainers. All that should be required is a suitable choker collar and a light lead, both of which may be made cheaply and effectively from a length of plastic washing line. A check cord some 20 or 30 yards (18.3 m or 27.4 m) long made from a length of cord, or powerful fishing line, is also necessary in the early stages. Some dummies, most of them easily made from stout canvas, or from old stockings, are all that should be needed otherwise. At some stage access to a pigeon loft is also useful. Otherwise the trainer may like to use a blank pistol for initially teaching the drop to shot, or may simply use blanks, or ordinary cartridges, in a shotgun, which is probably just as good. The simpler all methods of training can be kept generally the better.

2 Initial Obedience Training

In training a puppy the trainer is in effect faced with the problem of programming a computer which is alive and has a mind and will of its own. The object is to establish two way communication with the pup and achieve a mutual understanding with it. To attain any degree of success it is essential that the trainer knows before starting exactly what it is desired to teach the pup and how the process is best accomplished. Without a definite training programme decided beforehand, without the aids firmly fixed in the trainer's mind from the start, as well as the likeliest methods of achieving them, along with the answers to possible problems, it is fairly obvious that any good results will owe more to the abilities of the pupil than the expertise of the handler.

The object of the initial obedience training is to teach the pup to recognise and respond to its name, to come to heel when called by command, whistle, or signal. It must also learn to sit and stay to command, signal, or whistle. It must learn to accept the collar and lead and walk with them, or without them, at heel, sitting when the trainer halts. It must also recognise the universal prohibition 'No' and the word 'On' when it is released from a command. All this may seem a great deal for initial training, but when it is considered that it is in effect covered by two commands, 'Sit' and 'Heel', the prohibition 'No' and the encouragement 'On', it is not in fact so very much to expect.

The important point is always, throughout the entire training, to keep the commands, whistles and signals to a minimum and avoid confusion, or duplication. Above all it is desirable to avoid confused and unnecessarily wordy commands such as 'Come here. Come to heel'. All that is required is the single command 'Heel' at most prefaced by the pup's name, or a short prefatory warning whistle, to draw its attention to the coming command. By keeping commands short, while making sure, firmly but gently, that they are obeyed, and by regular repetition, stopping short of boredom, the pup will soon understand what is required of it.

Once the pup has arrived at its new home the process of acclimatisation should be continued in the same manner as indicated in the previous chapter. Unless soiled, any bedding which may have come with it should be mixed with the fresh bedding in its bed, or fresh bedding rubbed over the pup to acquire its scent. Alternatively, if the pup is being kept in the house it should be introduced to its special cupboard, or basket, where a blanket should be rubbed over it to provide it with a familiar scent on which to lie. In either case a further bone, or plaything, should also be provided to keep it interested and occupied. As a matter of course the puppy should be offered food and water, although initially it will probably be too excited and bewildered to eat or drink much.

It is important to remember that to a very small puppy a normal sized man must seem a vast object towering above it like an omnipotent being. When a hand is raised, or extended towards it, such a gesture may well be misinterpreted by the pup as a menacing threat. In the same way the voice even slightly raised may seem less than encouraging. It is extremely important to remember at all times how much tone of voice can mean to a small pup, or for that matter a mature dog. It is desirable therefore at least while the pup is young to avoid sudden careless gestures and to control the tone of voice with care.

At this stage it is important to remember that the pup is literally a baby. It does not even know its name. It has to be taught everything and its powers of concentration are not exactly very great. Nor is it able to communicate its wishes. It is entirely up to the owner to train it to do what he desires. This can only be done gradually with patience and by sticking to a set routine in certain matters. It is surprising, however, how much can be achieved in a comparatively short time. Even in the first few days the pup is likely to make very considerable advances as it settles into its new home.

After the pup's arrival at its new home and the introduction to its kennel, or basket, followed by its first meal, or meals, the first major problem is likely to be that of leaving it alone for the night. If it has a kennel companion to provide company for it there is usually little or no problem, although introducing the newcomer to an older dog may on occasions present difficulties. In practice, although the pup may start by being playful it will usually abase itself at once if an older dog expresses displeasure, and there is generally not much trouble about the acceptance of the newcomer.

To hasten the procedure it may be worth rubbing the pup all over with a blanket, or straw, in which the older dog normally sleeps, thus providing it with a familiar scent. Only when the older dog evinces extreme jealousy and attacks the newcomer is it perhaps advisable to keep them separate for the night. In very extreme cases it may even be necessary to kennel them separately, although this is unusual. The very fact that the pup has a companion in the kennel, even if separated from him by a partition, will, however, probably help to keep it reasonably quiet and content.

Where the pup is by itself it must be remembered that it has been abruptly separated from its familiar litter companions and from its mother and it is bound to feel lonely. Wherever it is left it will probably howl in its misery. The best solution is either to get the vet to prescribe a tranquilliser pill in advance, or to feed it half an aspirin in a last drink of warm milk prior to kennelling it for the night. After it has relieved itself, it should then be put firmly to bed, having ensured that it is comfortable and reasonably warm in its kennel, or basket, and on no account should it be visited again until morning, however much it may howl. At the very most a firm 'No' from outside the kennel, or room containing the basket is all that should be conceded, but even that is undesirable.

This may sound like a heartless attitude, but the fact remains that if the pup is visited when it howls it will decide that this is the way to get company and attention. It will therefore probably howl even louder until it is visited again. A determined pup can quite easily keep this up until in despair the misguided owners let it out. The pup will then have won its first battle of wills with its new owners and from then on will probably end up in their bedroom, if not in their bed.

Assuming that this particular trial of strength has either been avoided altogether by tactful handling, or by the administration of a tranquilliser, or else successfully overcome, the pup will from then on associate its kennel, or basket, with a refuge. It is there it will naturally retreat for safety when frightened, or when seeking rest, and it is there it will take any cherished bones, or playthings. This is a natural reaction which can be utilised by the trainer in the early days with considerable effect.

If working alone the trainer should get between the pup and its kennel, or basket, but it is preferable to have an assistant to hold the pup in a suitable position. Then all that is required is for the trainer to bend down, or squat, slightly turned away from the pup, and call it by name. The reason for being slightly turned away is twofold, in that the trainer's eyes, which often have a cowing effect on a puppy, may be averted and also so that the pup automatically arrives at the correct heel position. Rather than inadvertently adding to the name what from the pup's viewpoint are merely the confusing sounds 'Come here', it is far better to add the command 'Heel' from the start. It is a matter of choice for the individual trainer how soon this is added, but its use from the beginning does no harm, if only by checking any tendency towards careless commands.

When released the pup's natural instinct to run towards its place of refuge will ensure that it comes directly to the trainer, whereupon it should be held gently in the heel position. It should be praised immediately, stroked and possibly given a scrap of meat, or biscuit, although it is undesirable to reward it in this way too often in case it comes to expect it. The same performance may be repeated with the trainer and assistant possibly changing roles, but take care not to overdo it, even if the lesson is largely treated as a game. By using its name at every opportunity, when calling it, praising it, or at meals, the pup will soon learn to respond to it.

It is not too much to expect an intelligent pup addressed by name at every suitable opportunity to be responding well to it within two or three days. From the very start when bending down, or squatting, to urge the pup to come, the trainer should also pat the knee, or lower leg, as further encouragement. The pup will soon come to associate this signal with the command to come.

As soon as the pup is answering confidently to its name the next advance may be made. The command 'Heel', if it has not already been used, should be added, whenever the pup is called. On coming to the trainer the pup should always be guided into the correct heel position. Whenever it fails to arrive at the correct heel position from the start the pup should consistently be placed, gently but firmly, in the right place. It should also, of course, be stroked and verbally praised for its response to the command and signal. Once again it is not likely to be very long before an intelligent pup is responding perfectly to its name, the command 'Heel' and the signal of the hand patting the knee, or lower leg.

In addition to the signal of patting the knee, or lower leg, and calling its name, followed by the command 'Heel', whatever whistle is to be used may also be added at this stage. Although, at least in theory, any whistle, or for that matter any musical instrument, would do, the most convenient is probably a repeated short whistle, a series of short notes, which cannot readily be mistaken for any other whistle and which can be heard from a distance with ease. By gradually adding this whistle, after the name and command 'Heel' along with the hand signal when calling the pup it should soon be coming very confidently to all three. From then on it is up to the trainer to vary the sequence by using the command, whistle, or signal in different order, or by omitting one, or more. Thus the pup should soon be responding happily to its name and the command, whistle, or signal alone, or any combination.

From the first the feeding routine should also be associated with the pup's name, thus using its stomach to assist in its training. Standing between the pup and its kennel, or basket, the trainer should squat down and call the pup's name while holding the food dish towards it to add the smell to the general encouragement to come. As the pup approaches, the trainer should raise the dish slightly so that the pup has to come to a stop and look up at it, probably sitting involuntarily as it does so. The trainer should encourage this by placing a hand gently on the loins, at the same time placing the dish in front of it and saying firmly 'Sit'.

Immediately following the command 'Sit', the whistle which will be used to accompany it should also be given. While in theory again any whistle would do, it obviously has to be as different from the whistle meaning 'Heel' as possible and it is probably best to use one prolonged note, which can be easily distinguished and heard at a distance. The pup should meanwhile be restrained briefly from rushing foward with the hand on the loins holding it back and the all embracing command 'No'. After a moment or so's delay, while the pup is gently held back, it may be released with a wave of the hand forward and the acknowledgement 'On'.

This performance repeated four times a day, or as often as it is decided to feed the pup at this stage, will very quickly help to induce an eager response to the name as well as an understanding of these various commands and whistles. Very soon the two sets of commands may be used in conjunction. The name and the call whistle, with, or without, the command 'Heel' and the hand signal, may be followed by the command 'Sit' and prolonged whistle, so that the pup is brought to heel and sitting. It may then be waved forward to the feed bowl, with the affirmative acknowledgement 'On' encouraging it to go forward to eat. Any attempt to rush forward prior to permission being given must, of course, be restrained with the universal prohibition 'No'. It should only be a matter of a few weeks before the pup can be called to the heel position and will sit to any combination of commands, whistles, or signals.

It is important, however, not only for the pup to understand all the commands, whistles and signals, but for the trainer and anyone working as assistant, or in contact with the pup, to realise their fuller implications. Thus the command 'Sit' also signifies 'Stay', although at this stage this aspect of the training has not been begun. It is therefore important whenever the pup has been made to sit to command or whistle, or later to signal, that it should be given the affirmative acknowledgement 'On' and a forward wave, and click of the fingers, when it is expected to move forward at heel. When the heel command is abandoned again the affirmative 'On' may be used to show that the command no longer applies. In fact 'On' is in many ways the opposite of 'No' since it signifies at this stage release from a command and permission to go forward. It is a combination of 'Go on' and 'Right'. Later it will be used to send the dog forward to quarter and as encouragement to work even later in the training. It might be considered as a general affirmative and release from command at this stage.

The command 'Heel', as has been seen, covers numerous wordy commands such as 'Come here' and 'Come to heel'. Although at this stage only used when the trainer is bending down, or squatting, it will later be used when walking, after the lead training has been introduced. Once the two commands 'Heel' and 'Sit' are fully understood the pup in due course will usually be expected to sit whenever called to heel, but in these early stages it should not be allowed to get away with anticipating a command. Should this happen the command ought still be given, even if the pup in this case is already sitting. When the pup is under instruction, as opposed to playing, the trainer should as far as possible control all its actions by command. When it is released from the lesson the affirmative 'On' and forward wave with a click of the fingers should signify the fact.

The command 'No' as the universal prohibition is soon understood, but it is very important that the pup understands whenever it has done, or attempted to do, something meriting prohibition. Frequently it is difficult, if not impossible, for the pup to understand what it has done wrong, although it is aware that somehow it has transgressed. It is always best, if possible, for the trainer to think ahead of the pup, like a driver 'reading' the road ahead, and check any wrong doing in advance with a warning 'No'.

Thus early house training may be taught quite painlessly by ensuring that after every occasion when the pup has had a drink of water it is put outside until it has relieved itself. Any attempt to relieve itself inside the house should be checked at once with a firm 'No' and immediate removal outside. On every occasion it is taken outside and relieves itself correctly it should be praised accordingly. Properly conducted, house training may mean some intensive pup watching for a brief period, but it should only last a short time and ideally the pup will not be given any opportunities to make mistakes.

The importance of warmth in the sleeping area is important in this respect. If the pup does not have enough bedding in its kennel to keep it warm, or if its basket is in a draught, it may catch a chill. If it is cold, or catches a chill, mistakes early on are not easily avoided and can scarcely be blamed on the pup. Also if the pup is not put out at regular intervals it cannot be expected to abstain from relieving itself. Punishment long after the event may not be associated with the crime. Unless caught in the act any punishment may merely confuse the pup and cause further trouble.

This is one of the comparatively simple lessons which, if things go wrong, as they very easily can, may take very much longer to inculcate than might be believed possible. A moment's thoughtless heavy handedness may cause a lot of trouble. It may even be that the pup gets the wrong idea and thinks that it is supposed to relieve itself indoors rather than outside. Be careful therefore about any form of punishment for this offence. Here, indeed, prevention is better than cure.

With defecation the same principles apply. The pup should be put out in its run immediately after feeding. Subsequently it should be exercised outside until it has cleared its bowels. If a mistake is made it should be sufficient to show it the offending faeces and give the universal prohibition 'No' at the same time putting the pup outside. A few repetitions in most cases and the lesson will be learned. It must be added, however, that some dogs and some breeds are naturally clean and hardly ever, even as pups, transgress in this fashion, while others, unfortunately, are not so reliable. Even in such cases, however, it is only a matter of time and perserverance before, to use an apt phrase, 'the penny drops'.

Regularity in feeding, in training and in household routine all helps the pup to settle down and become acclimatised more quickly. From the start, whether the pup is kept in the kennel, or in the house, it should have its day regularly divided into sections when it knows it may expect certain events to take place. It should look forward to meal times and exercise periods and to its daily lessons and know when to expect them, for in such matters regularity is desirable as far as possible. If it is kept in the kennel, of course, this is usually very much simpler than if it is kept in the house.

If it is kept in the house it may have to adapt itself to a rather more varied household routine, but once again it must be emphasised that it should have its own kennel area, even if this consists only of a basket in a corner, where it is expected to withdraw on the appropriate command of 'Kennel' or 'Basket'. It must be obvious that in these circumstances a dark cupboard, or screened alcove, to which it can retire is much preferable. Here, as in an outside kennel, it should be entitled to security and privacy, away from children, bright lights, television, or other distractions, which might prevent it having the sound sleep it requires. Here it should not be interfered with by anyone, although, as with the kennel, the basket should be cleaned daily.

All of this is not to say that the pup should not be allowed, indeed, encouraged to play and enjoy life as a puppy should. The trainer should encourage it to play and have games with him. It is just as important that it should romp off its high spirits and enjoy its puppyhood as that it should learn obedience. Indeed it is desirable that the pup should have its own toys, or playthings, such as a rubber bone, or ring, preferably something fairly solid which will help it when it comes to teething. This sort of thing will give it something to chew, rather than attacking the kennel fittings, its basket, or other items such as shoes.

Throughout these early days and for the first six months or more of the pup's life these commands, whistles and signals should be used daily and always gently but firmly enforced if necessary, as a means of communicating with the pup. There should, however, never be anything heavy handed about this. It should never, for instance, be necessary to strike a pup and tone of voice should always be enough to demonstrate disapproval. Thus the early lessons, like the house training, should ideally evolve as a result of the trainer's actions and these communications, rather than being consciously taught. If the various commands and signals are quietly and regularly enforced without stress and never used incorrectly the pup should continue to learn daily without real, or conscious, effort. In effect the trainer should be increasing daily the communication and understanding between them.

As far as possible it is desirable to keep the lessons, as such, to a minimum. While certain brief periods of say a quarter of an hour or so may be set aside daily for lessons these should never be over stressed. They may consist of only one action casually performed as a matter of course during a short outing. On the other hand those commands already learned should automatically be carried out where required as a matter of course, but never in such a way as to allow them to seem boring and thus encourage the pup to introduce variety by disobeying them.

Thus the pup should be absorbing the meaning of the various commands, signals and whistles and obeying them, while taking pleasure and pride in doing so. As long as it is continuing to strive to please and the trainer is merely channelling its instincts and actions, while continuing daily to broaden its abilities and understanding of what is required, the relationship is perfect. It is up to the trainer with his greatly superior intellect to keep matters that way, but, of course, it is not always so simple.

The important point is to gauge the right time for each new approach and at any signs of resistance, or refusal to cooperate, to distract the pup's attention and finish that particular session. By constant variety and tiny advances at a time the training should progress steadily and it is surprising how much can be achieved. The trainer has to study the pup and constantly keep broadening its experience as well as maintaining obedience.

One of the earlier and more important lessons, for example, is the introduction of the puppy to a lead. A very light lead is, of course, desirable in the first instance. A suitable light choker lead for this purpose may be made easily and cheaply from a length of plastic clothes line. Some people may favour putting a collar on the pup at this stage, but it seems to me that this is merely adding an unnecessary extra dimension to a simple lesson. In practice if the pup has a light plastic, or leather, choker lead slipped over its head and is distracted from what is happening by the offer of a toy while the lead is dangled so that no pressure is on its neck, some moments will probably pass before it even realises that the lead is in position. As soon as it starts to do so the lead can then be removed and the first lesson, namely putting on the collar and lead, should have been painlessly accepted. The pup is praised and probably is not even fully aware of quite what has happened.

Thereafter, on the next suitable occasion, the lead may be slipped on without trouble and the pup allowed to play around, ambling after a toy, without any pressure being put on it. It may even be possible to encourage the pup to follow across the room without any restraint on its neck. That again should be enough. Once more the lead is removed and put away and the pup is duly praised. The next time some slight restraint may be applied and the command 'Sit' given. Once this has been obeyed the lead may be slipped off and the pup praised yet again. The next stage has been learned. Thereafter the pup may well take quite happily to the lead with no further need to train it. Lead training can very often be as painless as that.

On the other hand, if the trainer is heavy handed and initially goes on too long there may well be resistances. The pup may fight the lead, roll on its back, or retreat and do its best to strangle itself. Although they should never have been allowed to arise in the first place, such exhibitions should be treated firmly with the prohibition 'No' and a slight jerk on the lead. The command 'Sit' may follow and, once obeyed, the lead might be removed. When the pup appreciates that nothing is to be gained by misbehaviour it will very quickly accept the inevitable. Only if the trainer is weak enough to give way or insists on a real confrontation is there likely to be real trouble.

If the pup learns that behaviour such as that mentioned results in it getting its own way the whole training programme is endangered. In practice, however, confrontations, even minor ones, are always to be avoided whenever possible, if only because they indicate a breakdown in communication. It is almost always possible to distract the pup's attention so that the lesson is at least half learned before it has been realised what is happening. It is usually only when the trainer has made a mistake that emergency measures are required, but in such cases it is almost always best to bring the lesson quickly to a conclusion and finish as far as possible with some simple command obeyed. Then give the pup time to forget the event and next time use a different approach.

Once the pup has become accustomed to the lead it is usually no trouble to fasten a collar round its neck as and when required before going out. The pup soon associates the collar and lead with an outing and is pleased to see them. The lead and choker collar are thereafter a part of the general training programme. When the pup goes for a walk on the collar and lead it should automatically, from the first, be walked at heel, held firmly in the desired position with one hand holding the lead behind the trainer's back and the other ready to twitch briefly if the position is not maintained. This is, however, a lesson quickly learned and the use of a wall, or fence, to maintain the heel position makes for simplicity in the early days.

From having previously been largely static the lessons can now be conducted on the move. Furthermore the pup now has to learn when to obey unspoken commands. For instance while walking with the pup on the lead at heel whenever the trainer stops the pup should sit automatically. Initially it will be necessary to give the command, or a signal, but as indicated earlier this is a reaction which comes very naturally. Just the same the pup should still be praised for its obedience to an unspoken command on such occasions. A sharp eye should also be kept on the pup until his reaction has become automatic.

It is surprising how quickly a young pup can learn these initial lessons. At this stage, or whenever it is felt the pup is sufficiently mature, it is desirable to add two signals to the command 'Sit' and the long whistle. These are the obvious raised hand of the traffic policeman, which is easily seen from a distance and is useful to make the pup sit when neither whistle, nor command are suitable. The other is the stamped foot, which can also be seen from a surprising distance, but is usually used at fairly close quarters when the hands are otherwise occupied, with gun or other paraphernalia. It is not usually a good idea to start with these too early on as they are inclined to have an inhibiting effect on sensitive pups.

Any other gestures, or signals, could, of course, be used. Indeed it would be perfectly feasibly to teach the pup to sit whenever the trainer bowed, or sat, just as a horn might be used instead of a whistle, but for convenience sake the raised hand and stamped foot are probably the most emphatic and useful. Added to the command 'Sit' and the long whistle these two will soon be recognised and obeyed by themselves. If either is used too early with a sensitive pup, however, it might easily be frightened, causing an undesirable setback to the training.

It is always important to try to gauge the pup's likely reactions to any training in advance. Sometimes it may even be wiser to dispense with any training whatever if the pup shows signs of being a little off-colour, due for instance to teething, worms, a chill, or any of the other common ailments pups do suffer from even in the best regulated kennels. If there are any signs of the pup not performing as well as usual this may easily be due to the onset of something of this nature.·

As a matter of course the pup's condition should always be noted first thing in the morning. It is inexcusable to miss the symptoms of illness and it should be automatic to make a daily, even if unconscious, check on your animal's health. After a while it should become second nature to take in at a glance the state of the pup's coat, noting at once that it is smooth and glossy, not harsh or staring. The eye should be lively and bright, not weeping, or dull. The nose should be moist, not dry and hot. The faeces should be reasonably solid and healthy, not unduly moist or evil smelling. The pup should not be straining over them, or when passing water. These are the obvious points.

In addition the pup should be lively and pleased to see you, not dull and listless. Its movements should be easy and even, not in any way cramped, or halting, indicating either a stomach upset, or a back or loin injury, or foot, hip, or shoulder lameness. Any signs of worms, undue licking of the anus, dragging the bottom on the ground, or remnants in the faeces, should be spotted at once. Any undue scratching, irritation of the skin, or undue shaking and flapping of the ears may indicate the presence of mites, or fleas, or possibly canker. In such cases a visit to the vet may be called for, but in any event the reason for the pup's lack of condition should promptly be ascertained and remedial action taken.

With every pup it is also vitally important to gauge just how much training it can stand. As with the adolescent who grows in fits and starts, so it is probable that the pup will progress quite splendidly for a period and then, for no obvious reason, will appear, at least by comparison, to stagnate for a while. Even the cleverest of pups, which seems to understand every lesson, will suddenly have periods when nothing goes right. In any such case it is important at once to ease off the training, for otherwise almost certainly matters will merely deteriorate.

It is here that professional trainers with a number of pups to train are at something of an advantage over the amateur. They can only afford to give a small amount of individual time to each pup daily, but the pups benefit from the power of example and when not being taught they have each other for company and play. Furthermore the professionals know what they are aiming for and can watch various pups and make comparions between them, which can often be very helpful. They can then concentrate on the ones needing most care and let the natural developers set their own pace.

The amateur, on the other hand, with only one pup has the advantage that it can be given individual attention. If this is overdone, of course, it can lead to trouble, especially if the pup is forced beyond its abilities. On the other hand if the amateur trainer has a full time job which takes up most of each day it may not be easy to spare the necessary time to train the pup. Either before starting work, or on returning, the trainer must still try to give the pup an individual lesson each day, even if it is only a very short one. At the weekends a further lesson, or even two, may be added, but the really important thing is to try to maintain a regular schedule, rather than work in fits and starts with intensive sessions at weekends, which can easily lead to a bored pup.

From the first it is important to try to foster the impression that there is an invisible bond of control between the pup and the trainer. It is desirable to let the pup run free, but it is equally important that it should drop to command, or whistle, and come to heel when called. It is always unwise therefore to give careless commands that cannot be enforced. If the pup does not come at once when called a sharp change of direction will probably bring it running. Then a quick word of praise should be given and the lead slipped into place. As far as possible the pup should never be allowed to appreciate that it has been successfully disobedient, even where that has been the case.

If the pup develops a resistance to coming to heel, perhaps because it has been at some point unwisely reprimanded on coming, it should never be coerced, or worst still chased. If an abrupt change of direction on the trainer's part does not work, it is advisable to get between it and its kennel and intercept it. If the pup gets to its kennel first, it should be placed in the heel position, with the command 'Heel' repeated. Then it might be wise to take a short walk with it at heel on the lead before returning to the kennel and praising it.

Where for some reason the steady and progressive approach to training advocated has been interrupted and, as suggested above, the pup has developed a resistance to coming to heel, or where a headstrong and impetuous pup has been acquired at the age of several months, it may pay to slip on the check cord. The pup should then be given an opportunity to repeat its disobedience. If it is then bowled head over heels with a sudden jerk of the cord no harm will be done, but a sharp lesson will have been taught. The idea has been implanted in its mind that the trainer has a mysterious ability to enforce commands at a distance, which is all to the good.

The ground for this lesson should be carefully prepared when the time is judged right and it should not be overdone, or the pup will soon learn the meaning of the check cord and obey perfectly when it is on, but continue its disobedience when it is running free. The trainer, however, should always try to avoid confrontations of this kind, especially over small issues, hence the importance of only giving a few commands and making sure, as far as possible, that they are obeyed. Even where there is disobedience it is usually far better to ignore it and ensure that a command is finally obeyed, rather than impress on the pup's mind the negative lesson that it can disobey with impunity. It is worth trying whenever possible to end any lesson on a good note.

There are two very important points to remember, especially with a very young pup. One is that it should never be over-exercised, as this can easily cause a weak heart or other ailments to develop, and the other is that the limit of concentration is not long. No-one would expect a baby, or a very young child, to concentrate for any length of time before becoming bored, or distracted, and the same thing applies to dogs. When the pup starts behaving in an unusually tiresome, or difficult manner, this may not be so much a sign of disobedience, or incipient sickness, as of boredom. The trainer should always bear this possibility in mind and try to avoid it.

It cannot be over-stressed that it is extremely important at every stage of training to avoid boring the pup. Always following the same routine, so that the pup begins to anticipate the lesson, is a sure way to build a resistance to the lessons resulting in disobedience. Understandably, in the circumstances, the pup will become mutinous, refusing to obey perfectly simple orders, or otherwise evincing every sign of boredom. The only solution is probably to suspend training altogether for a few days and then start a completely new and more varied series of lessons. As is usually the case when things go wrong, it is the trainer, not the pup, at fault.

OUTLINE OF POSSIBLE TRAINING SCHEDULE: INITIAL STAGE

First week:

Day 1:   Return with pup: Introduce and acclimatise to kennel outside and basket inside: Feed evening meal, using name: Successfully perform 'Sit': Briefly use universal prohibition 'No' and affirmative 'On' with click of fingers and forward wave of hand and arm: Feed half aspirin in warm milk and kennel: Do not respond to howls.

Day 2: At each meal call by name and 'Heel', with brief repeated whistle and signal of hand tapping knee: Use 'Sit', 'No' and 'On' with wave of hand.

Day 3: At each meal in addition to 'Sit', give prolonged whistle: Twice call towards basket, or kennel, by name with repeated short whistle, and hand signal tapping knee, with command 'Heel', intercept and praise: Should be starting to recognise name.

Day 4: Meals routine: Name, 'Heel', whistle, 'Sit', whistle, 'No' and 'On'. Should be responding to name and sitting at meals: Understanding routine: Also should be beginning to respond to command 'Heel', signal and whistle.

Day 5: Meal routine as above: Twice get between pup and basket, or kennel, call name, whistle, 'Heel' and signal: Vary order by using name, then whistle and signal, finally 'Heel'.

Day 6: Two extra short lessons over weekday routine: Try name and whistle, with signal to come to heel: Next time name 'Heel' and whistle: Try whistle alone: Vary with signal to come to heel and whistle to 'Sit' when comes.

Day 7: Two extra sessions on coming to heel to command and whistle: Name should now be fully recognised and should be starting to respond to commands whistles and signals.

Second Week: Continue variations as for First Week. Third Week: Should now understand name, commands 'Heel' and 'Sit', 'No' and 'On', also accompanying signals and whistles:

Day 1: Meal rountine; still four times daily: Twice daily lessons, of ten minutes: Varied commands, signals and whistles: Lead slipped on briefly and removed before noticed.

Day 2: During varied routine of whistles, commands, signals lead twice slipped on and second time led a few paces before noticed.

Day 3:   Lesson routine varied. At sit lead placed on and removed: No notice taken: Remained sitting obediently without moving.

Day 4:   Lessons varied and lead slipped on for several paces: Then made to sit to command: Lead removed.

Day 5:   Lead slipped on at start of lesson and when noticed led step or two then made to sit: Lead removed: Signals, commands, whistles varied.

Day 6:   Lesson routine varied, but lead work increased: No notice now taken and responding quite happily: Commands, signals and whistles: Walk at heel on lead: Double lessons.

Day 7:   Double lessons again: Pup quite accustomed to lead and now able to go walk outside: Two different walks: Different routines: Lead removed and pup allowed to roam, but only restricted exercise.

Fourth Week: Much simpler to vary lesson routines with use of lead: Different route taken each day as well as varied routine for lessons: Raised hand and stamped foot now introduced with command 'Sit', but this dependant on pup's reactions.

Fifth Week: Now walking well on lead and responding to unspoken commands. Sitting automatically when halted on lead: Walking at heel following use of wall and fence to maintain position: Responds to name, commands, signals and whistles: Pleased to see lead and happy to have it put on, or taken off. Lessons still restricted to ten minutes and walks no more than quarter of an hour: Pup should not be over-exercised.

Sixth Week: Pup should now know name well: Respond to commands 'Heel' and 'Sit', understand 'No' and 'On', with wave of hand, or clicked fingers: Will sit to long whistle and come to heel to short repeated whistle: Will come to heel when hand tapped against leg: Also sits to raised hand or stamped foot: It will come to heel and sit automatically when called: It will walk on the lead maintaining heel position and enjoys having lead put on or removed: If there is any problem at this stage the use of the check cord may be the answer: The pup will be roaming further away and should not be curbed when it does so, but changes of direction ought to make it keep an eye on the trainer. Although the pup should be allowed to roam freely, exercise must not be overdone at this age: By this time house training should be perfect.

Seventh and Eighth Weeks: Lessons continued as indicated with constant variety: It may be that a slow pup will require this amount of time to reach the standard outlined: Equally a very forward pup may have been quicker: Each pup and trainer will be different.

3 Initial Obedience Training: Secondary Stage

In the initial obedience training so far, the pup has learned to answer to its name, to come to heel when called in answer to the command 'Heel' prefaced by its name, or to the signal of the hand tapping against the knee, or lower leg, or to the repeated short whistle. It will obey the command 'Sit' and will also sit to the prolonged whistle and the raised hand, or stamped foot. It is already lead trained and will obediently walk at heel on the lead, sitting when the trainer halts without command. It is fully house trained.

From this stage onwards the important thing is to keep continually broadening its horizons and general experience. It must be taught to accept the car as a means of transport. It must learn to behave in public amongst other people and amongst other dogs, in both town and country. It must learn to obey commands obediently despite distractions close at hand. It should be taught to cross obstacles when told to do so, but not to break fence (i.e. to cross a fence without orders) It must be taught to drop automatically at a distance to the whistle, or command, or signal. It should be taught that when commanded to 'Sit' this also means 'Stay'. It should be introduced to the gun and taught to drop to shot. It may also be taught to drop to the sight of flushed ground game. It should also be taught to enter water and swim without fear. It may be that during this training period it has also started both pointing and retrieving.

Undoubtedly the most important lesson of all its training is teaching the pup to sit at a distance. The 'long drop', to whistle, signal, or command, is central to all subsequent training. Also important is the introduction to shot. It is not only important that the pup should learn to accept shots as an ordinary part of the daily routine, but it should also learn to drop to the sound of shot automatically. In the same way it should also learn to drop to the flush of game automatically. All these points can be suitably brought into this secondary stage of the initial obedience training.

In addition to all this, the lessons already learned in the first stage of the initial obedience training should be repeated until they become second nature. It is on the foundations already laid that the rest of the training depends. Those lessons already learned should gradually be extended, so that, for instance, the pup walks happily at heel with, or without, the lead and whether close to a wall, or fence, or in the open. Throughout the secondary stage of the initial obedience training the pup's abilities and experience should be expanded steadily to provide a thoroughly sound basis for its advanced training as a working gundog.

From the moment that the pup is lead trained and starting to be obedient to simple commands, particularly the universal prohibition 'No', it is important, for instance, to take it out to meet other people and other dogs and generally introduce it to the outside world. If a pup is kept in its own kennel all the time without seeing other people, or other dogs, or indeed anything beyond the immediate vicinity of its run, it is not surprising if it becomes easily frightened, or responds by growling, or barking, at strange sights. In extreme cases, where the pup has been kept permanently secluded, it can develop neurotic tendencies, such as running away and hiding at the sight of a stranger.

Inevitably, as a working gundog, the pup will eventually have to become accustomed to meeting strange dogs and getting into strange Land Rovers and cars with other people, along with their dogs. If it is not completely used to this sort of thing and if it barks, or growls, at other dogs, or worse still fights, it will be a thorough nuisance to all concerned and the owner will not be at all popular. Since all that is required is to accustom the pup from the earliest days to meeting others there is really no excuse for this quite common failing.

It is, in any event, important to introduce the pup to the car early on and adequate 'car training' should be a normal part of every youngster's education, although this does not always seem to be the case. Anyway, from quite early days, the pup should be taken along in the car whenever it is convenient to do so. On the first few occasions this may mean someone accompanying it with suitable supplies of newspaper, in case it is car-sick. Even where the pup is not a good traveller initially this should wear off quite soon and then it will begin to look forward eagerly to car journeys.

A great deal, of course, depends on the type of car and where the pup is expected to travel. Ideally it should be accustomed from the start to various types of car, from saloons, to hatchbacks and estates. In each case it is obviously desirable to decide where and how the pup will travel and once the decision is made to try to keep to it. If it is to travel in a saloon it may be allowed on the back seat, in which case it should, preferably, have its own rug, or travelling basket, provided. Alternatively it may be expected to travel on the floor, if necessary under the feet of the passenger in front, or behind. In a hatchback, or estate car, the pup should be restricted to the rear area, but again with its own rug, or basket. Whatever method is decided on should be maintained from the start, for there are few things worse than a dog roaming all round a car, as well as the hazard involved.

There are those who advocate having the dog in the boot of a saloon in a travelling kennel. Specially designed grills can be bought to keep the boot wedged slightly open to provide air. It is highly desirable, however, with this method, or when a dog is travelling in the back of a hatchback, or estate car, to ensure that the exhaust fumes are carried clear of the car and are not funnelling into the rear space as can easily happen. In particularly bad cases the dog could be asphyxiated, but even small doses can leave an animal at least temporarily deaf.

It is quite common, although obviously dangerous, to see a dog travelling in a car with its head out of the window. Apart from the obvious possibility of the dog having its head hit by another car, this is likely to result in ear canker, or eye strain. A far worse fault, however, is to allow a dog to whine, or bark, in the car. Any such noisy exhibition should be checked at the first sign of it with a firm 'No'. There are few things more annoying when driving than a dog which is constantly whining, or barking, and it is a sign of extremely bad initial obedience training.

Although widely used, dog guards in estate cars, or hatchbacks, are on the whole not a particularly good thing, as the tendency is to rely on them and not to bother with car training. A dog guard should really be unnecessary if the trainer travels in the back seat on the first few occasions and restrains the pup with a firm 'No' every time it tries to leave the area chosen for it. If a dog guard is used the dog may later knock it down, or be in a car without one. It then becomes necessary to start the training at a time when bad habits may have already been formed and resistances to the training developed.

There are, however, inevitably occasions when it is necessary to leave the pup for quite long periods in the car and this should all be part of its training. It is preferable to avoid this if possible until the pup has attained a comparatively high standard in initial obedience training and can be relied upon to stay where it is told. Otherwise a dog guard may be necessary as a temporary measure, especially where food has to be left in the car, since to a young pup the temptation is then almost irresistible. The real answer in such circumstances should be for the trainer to remain in the car to check any attempt at transgression, for, if the pup cannot be relied on not to steal food, the only solution is to ensure that it has no chance to do so, but this is not always feasible.

Stealing food and scavenging are extremely tiresome vices which almost always go together, and once acquired are extremely hard to cure. In that a dog may unwittingly pick up and eat poisoned, or contaminated, food, which may make it extremely ill, or even kill it, these vices are highly undesirable. They may originate in insufficient or indifferent feeding, or be caused by ill-health, such as worms.

They can also be learned quite accidentally, as when visiting a house where they have the bad habit of leaving food lying about for the animals instead of removing the bowls as soon as they have eaten. The pup sees the food lying temptingly available and scoffs it quickly before it can be stopped. Alternatively the pup may come across a discarded sandwich, or similar tempting morsel, in a hedgerow, or beside a dustbin, and eat it before being seen. If such deeds go unnoticed and unchecked the pup has learned an extremely bad lesson. Thereafter the pup may sit obediently whenever food is placed in front of it and wait until it is told to eat with the affirmative 'On' and click of the fingers, but given the opportunity of eating any food lying around it will seize it shamelessly.

The best method of preventing this vice developing is to make sure that the pup has an opportunity to eat food which has been suitably prepared for it in advance. Thus a piece of bread soaked in bitter aloes, or a bread ball surrounding hot chilies, or better still a piece of tempting meat securely fixed to a springback mousetrap, set to frighten, not to catch the pup's nose, are all ways calculated to give it an immediate lesson that food should never be eaten unless it has permission to do so from the trainer. If the pup is forced to spit out the food it has seized, or if it gets a fright when it touches it, the lesson will be learned quickly, but some pups have amazing digestions and the mouse trap is probably the most certain method.

The treated food should be laid out where it is certain the pup will come across it and the prohibition 'No' should be given as soon as it is seen to grab it. If the pup obeys the order and spits out the food that is an indication that the training is going well, but the lesson may need repeating. If greed gets the better of it then the pup will learn a sharp lesson which will probably not need to be repeated. It should only be added that mustard sandwiches are not a suitable answer. I once laid out a set of mustard sandwiches and watched through the window as the dog they were prepared for ate the lot, smacked its lips and looked round for more. Once a dog has become a confirmed thief cures are difficult to say the least.

Inevitably the pup will also encounter patches of dung, the droppings of poultry and other birds, or similar excreta, as well as the rotting carcases of animals. It may well be that it starts to eat some of these and here, again, the universal prohibition 'No' must be firmly used and the pup led away from the spot, being made to understand it is in disgrace. It is difficult to prevent any pup indulging in such practices occasionally, but the cautionary training against theft should have its effect here. Should the pup continue to show evidence of a depraved appetite in this way it may be evidence of a need for a change in diet, or the pup may need worming. If it is desired at such a time, or any other, to do more than merely scold the pup a sharp shake by the scruff of the neck is quite sufficient at this stage accompanied by the prohibition 'No'.

Later on it may be permissible to bite the pup's ear by way of punishment, in the manner of the pack leader admonishing young, but beating with a stick, or hand, should never be necessary.

Although in general it is probably not desirable to take gundogs into other peoples' homes, or for that matter into hotels, public rooms, or shops, even where it is permitted to do so, this is undoubtedly an important part of the pup's education. It should be accustomed by degrees to the bustle of towns, to walking on crowded pavements, to entering crowded rooms, and sitting inconspicuously under its trainer's chair, or table, or beside its trainer's heel. Any attempt to stray away to investigate scents, or pull towards another dog, or a cat, or otherwise break lead discipline, must be firmly restrained at once with the prohibition 'No' and, if necessary, a twitch of the lead.

The crush of humanity, the strong smell of exhaust fumes, the chances of picking up disease, which is prevalent amongst a very high percentage of dogs in towns, are all reasons why these exercises should not be undertaken too often. On the other hand on a few regular occasions the pup should experience such conditions since they are an essential part of broadening its experience. In such surroundings it learns to stick closely to the trainer's heel and rely on him for safety and reassurance. In this respect, it is important not to forget to praise the pup if it obeys unspoken instructions by sitting when the trainer halts, or otherwise behaving well under what undoubtedly are extremely trying circumstances at the best of times.

Where there are neighbours with dogs of approximately the same age it is always desirable to introduce them and let them play together. If there are older dogs nearby it is also desirable to introduce them to the pup although more care is obviously necessary in such circumstances. In either case it is important to make sure that the pup does not learn any bad habits from the other dogs. Jealousy, whining, or barking, fighting, and disobedience of various kinds are easily learned in such circumstances unless care is taken at all times.

As well as accustoming the pup to the world of the town and to traffic, which in itself must be very frightening to any animal of that size, it is, of course, important to accustom it to country life and country diversions. As a part of its initial obedience training therefore it is advisable to lead the pup past fields of stock, from cattle to sheep and pigs. Naturally it is essential that at this stage it is kept on the lead for any attempt to chase would be undesirable, although at this age the likelihood is that the pup would be more frightened, even of sheep, than they of it. It should certainly not be allowed loose near cattle, or pigs, for either might seriously injure it. Any attempt to walk through a field of young bullocks, or cows with calves at foot, with a young dog can be a very tiresome experience and one that is very much better avoided.

The pup should also be introduced to poultry, from hens to geese, if they can be found locally, and it will probably sight-point in amazement at these strange animals. It should be kept on the lead on such occasions and it should certainly never be allowed any opportunity to give chase. In the spring or early summer there is always the chance of encountering fledglings, or a brood of young pheasant, or partridge, cheepers in the wild, but the prohibition 'No' should be applied to them as to poultry. It must also be applied to sheep, especially if the pup sees young lambs gambolling and shows a desire to join them at play. At this stage, however, it should be primarily a question of accustoming the pup to the sights and sounds of the country and giving it an idea of what it may encounter, rather than seriously training it not to chase. Just by familiarising it with these animals as part of the country scene the pup should learn to ignore them, especially as it comes to learn the excitement and interest of the work in store for it.

Other parts of the country scene with which the pup must become familiar are fences, hedges and ditches, in the same way that in the town it must become accustomed to swing doors, gutters and gratings, which also have their concealed hazards for innocent pups. Just as it is desirable that the pup should learn not to rush through doors ahead of its trainer, so it is desirable that it should not cross a fence, or hedge, before its trainer. 'Breaking fence', or 'Breaking field', which is the technical term for this misdeed, is a bad habit for the pup to acquire since later, when quartering ground, it might decide to cross a fence after an interesting scent and thus deprive its owner of a shot.

In the early days the pup will probably be baffled when it arrives at a fence. It should initially therefore either be lifted over, especially where there is any barbed wire, or be given the command 'Sit' and made to continue sitting while the trainer crosses the fence. The lower wires of the fence should be parted with the trainer's foot bearing down and making a hole for the pup to pass through, when the command 'Over' should be given. At this stage it is not desirable to urge the pup to go through a hedge, unless the trainer is able to go through in front of it, when again the pup should be made to sit before the command 'Over' is given. The time for hunting out thick hedges comes much later in the training programme.

When crossing ditches the trainer should make the pup sit and should cross the ditch first and then again the command 'Over' should be given. It is quite important incidentally to take care that the pup does not fall in. Apart from the fact that it may be difficult enough to retrieve the pup from some ditches it could give it a bad fright. This could be quite enough to put it off entering water, so it is advisable to have a care here too. These may all seem small points, but, as has been indicated, training a pup is made up of numerous small points from the sum of which the pup should benefit.

Of all the lessons that the pup is taught in its initial obedience training the most basic is undoubtedly the command 'Sit'. The pup has already learned to sit to command, whistle, and signals. The lesson must now be extended so that the pup will sit, or drop, without fail in the face of any distraction at a distance. This is the most important lesson in training any gundog, but especially any pointer-retriever. The long drop, as it is often termed, is the keystone of future training and work. Once this has been thoroughly mastered and has become second nature the rest of the training becomes comparatively simple.

Initially, when out walking, the pup should receive the command 'Sit'. The trainer should then withdraw several paces backwards, facing the pup, if necessary with the hand raised, to make the intention quite clear that the pup must remain sitting. When the trainer is at what is judged to be a sufficient distance the hand may be lowered, but, to prevent any movement from the pup it may be advisable for the foot to be stamped, or the command 'Sit' reiterated. After some moments the command 'Heel', hand signal, or whistle, may be given and the pup returned to heel and duly praised.

By gradually increasing the distance each day the trainer should soon be able to walk away as much as a hundred yards (91.4 m) or more without the pup offering to move. On occasions when the pup is then called to heel it may well be given the whistle, signals, or the command 'Sit' as it returns and it should at once drop. It may be held there for some time until either the trainer goes to it, or it is called to heel. In either case the trainer must praise the pup if it has responded well. If at any time it attempts to move without permission, or creeps forward, the prohibition 'No' should be loudly voiced and the command 'Sit' repeated. If it has moved it should be replaced firmly on the original spot, but it may be better to finish the lesson there and take it up another time. As with all lessons, the timing, place and sequence should be varied as much as possible to maintain the pup's interest.

It is desirable about this stage to teach the pup that 'Sit' also means 'Stay'. There are two ways of doing this, one rather more old fashioned than the other. In either case it is advisable to set the scene beforehand so that you can 'Sit' the pup in a place where it will not be disturbed and where you can watch without it being aware of the fact. A large room can serve the purpose, although an enclosed paddock, or walled garden, with a door is probably ideal. If in a room the pup should be tied firmly to the leg of a solid piece of furniture, such as a piano. Alternatively a long and very strong nylon fishing line may be tied to the pup's collar and run around the leg of furniture and led to the door, so that should the pup attempt to move towards the door a tug on the line will haul it sharply backwards. In a walled garden, or paddock, the same principle may be instituted, using a fence post instead of the piano leg. In either case the pup's behaviour can be watched without it knowing through the hinge of the door.

Once the pup has been placed in position with the command 'Sit', the trainer may withdraw through the doorway. From there he can observe the pup and since it should already have been trained to sit in the open for short periods while the trainer walks away there should not be any immediate reaction as he disappears from sight. Whenever the pup makes any attempt to move, however, it will either find itself held back by the post, or a firm tug should jerk it back into position. In either case the trainer may use his voice to good effect with the universal prohibition 'No'. The pup may be kept in that position for any length of time the trainer cares to stay behind the door, but anything over a quarter of an hour is likely to be enough. At any sign of movement the pup should, of course, receive a tug and the command 'No'. The old trainer's method in this case was to leave the pup tied to the spot to half strangulate itself for an hour or so and then regard it as beaten. The same results can be achieved quite painlessly by the methods indicated.

As noted at the start of the chapter, another of the important lessons in the secondary part of the initial obedience training is the introduction to the gun. If this is not conducted properly it can have disastrous effects on the pup and may set back the training for a considerable time. Yet usually it is simplicity itself. The best way to introduce the pup to shot is to choose a windy day and get an assistant to fire a shot well downwind. The pup's reactions should be watched and if it appears to need reassurance this should be given and that should be enough for the day.

With a pup of sound stock, however, the probability is that there will be practically no reaction whatever beyond an enquiring glance towards the sound. In this case the assistant may approach closer and fire one or two more shots, while the pup is made to sit, by command, whistle, or signal, immediately after each shot has been fired. Of course, if the pup shows any signs of fright, or alarm, the lesson should be left until a later date, when it is more mature. In practice with the assistant firing away from the pup downwind there should be no alarm shown at all. It is merely a question of using a tactful and sensible approach to the matter.

The really gun-shy dog is not so much born as made by man. Inept handling is almost certainly the cause of most so-called gun-shyness. It is almost always in fact gun nervousness, which has been caused by improper introduction to the gun. If a gun is fired in an enclosed space, as for instance out of a car window, the concussion inside is immense and should any pup be so unfortunate as to have some such experience as its first introduction, then gun nervousness is only to be expected. Similarly, if a slightly nervous pup has a gun fired directly over its head as its first introduction it is not surprising if thereafter it evinces a dislike of shots. The noise directly in front of a gun is vastly magnified. Who can blame any pup for being gun nervous in such circumstances?

In this connection it is worth noting that some people make the mistake of starting a pup with a .22 rifle, for this can prove very alarming to a sensitive pup. The whip crack of the rifle can clearly seem very frightening to animals. Similarly, blank shots, or dummy launchers, can also be surprisingly noisy and alarming, especially when fired close to the pup. Once accustomed to the twelve bore this is probably best of all, especially fired into the air. Whatever is fired it is always important to make sure there is no echo around for the early shots as this too can be alarming, greatly magnifying the sound. At this stage of the pup's development it is advisable to be careful about any matters concerning shooting. As with all aspects of training it is easy enough to make mistakes, but once a resistance has been set up in the pup's mind it is often extremely hard to overcome it.

It should be remembered, for instance, that while the trainer anyway may seem large and frightening to a small pup, when swinging a gun this impressioin must be much greater. The pup may think it is being threatened with a stick, or club. The gun can thus grow in its mind to seem a frightening object. The actual introduction to the gun, with the trainer simply carrying it, should therefore be gradual. Later the trainer may raise the gun and accustom the pup to seeing it swung around. Initially the gun and the shot need not be connected in the pup's mind at all. When the pup has grown accustomed to the gun being swung around near it, then acclimatised to the shot, or vice versa, it need only be later that the gun is actually shot over it. The important point is that the pup must learn by degrees to drop to shot as readily and immediately as it drops to whistle, signal, or command. This should gradually become a regular part of its training with the trainer carrying a gun. Thus when it comes to more advanced training the pup is well on its way to being steady to shot.

The trainer can now conveniently introduce the pup to the

rolling dummy. This is not intended for retrieving purposes, it is meant to resemble a running rabbit, or hare, and to tempt the pup to give chase. All that is required is an old croquet ball, with one or two cork-sized pieces of wood nailed to it and covered with rabbit, or roe skin, and a few rabbit, or hare, tails glued to it is ideal, but in fact any irregularly shaped small log, or even, at a pinch, a turnip, will do. If bowled downhill these will all travel quite a long way at speed, jumping and bouncing as they go. They provide a very tempting distraction very reminiscent of a running rabbit, or hare. It is useful to have an assistant hidden behind a hedge, or wall, downwind to bowl the dummy temptingly past within close range of the pup on the first few occasions, but in fact it is quite feasible, if the trainer choses the right moment, to manage this perfectly well alone.

On the first occasion the rolling dummy is used, if the trainer is at all doubtful of the pup, it is advisable to slip on the check cord and allow the pup to get some distance out before bowling the dummy past it. As soon as it has seen it, the drop whistle should be blown firmly. Should the pup offer to give chase a good jerk on the check cord will be enough and if the pup is rolled over it will do no harm. It will almost certainly not readily offer to give chase again. Thereafter, whenever the dummy is rolled past it in the open, the drop whistle should be blown and it should drop obediently, thus learning the all important lesson of dropping to the sight of flushed ground game. By way of variation the rolling dummy can be saluted with a shot fired in the air, but it should very quickly become automatic for the pup to drop at the sight of it bowling past.

The time has probably now come when it is no longer necessary, or even desirable, to give the pup its lessons in a quiet and secluded place. Increasingly the youngster should learn that it must concentrate on what is being taught and ignore any distractions that may arise. Thus the trainer should welcome occasional distractions during training, such as people walking past nearby, or stock moving close at hand, or even other dogs nearby. This is all good practice for the time later on when the pup will be working as a gundog with all sorts of distractions at hand.

Somewhere during this stage of the training, rather dependant on the weather and the time of year, the pup should be introduced to water. Like the introduction to the gun, this is another important hurdle in the pup's training, which is also easily enough surmounted, if the approach is gradual and sensibly graded. It is obviously undesirable, for instance, simply to pitch the wretched puppy into deep water and expect it to swim. It will, of course, do so, but it could well be put off entering water again of its own free will. All dogs can swim and most will take a delight in doing so, if properly introduced to it. When wrongly, or stupidly, introduced to it, however, even an incipiently excellent water dog may develop a very strong resistance to water.

As long ago as 1621 Gervase Markham, my favourite sporting author, in *The Whole Art of Fowling* recommended training a dog to retrieve from water by throwing a stone into a large tub with only a few inches of water in it. After it had been successfully retrieved he suggested adding a little more water by degrees until the dog had to dip its head under water to make the retrieve. In this way he reckoned to train a dog to dive under water after wounded wildfowl. He seems to have been an excellent animal trainer, even if not greatly worried about hard mouth, and the system he advocated of gradual progression was a sound one, far ahead of his day. Even with a natural water dog to expect results by simply urging the pup straight into water is asking for trouble.

It can sometimes take very little to put a dog off entering water. A pup I bred at one time, whose dam was an excellent water dog and whose progeny were also good, had a fright at some eighteen months caused by thin ice breaking while crossing a very small and shallow stream. At the time she seemed unaffected, but she soon showed an aversion to water. Although I was confident that she could easily be cured when the weather was warmer in the spring, she was sold in the interval. The new owner was warned that he should encourage her to overcome the fear by leading her into water in thigh boots, but he had no suitable water and as he bred from her some eighteen months later and the pup he kept proved a good water dog he never bothered to persevere with her. Thus, although she should have been first in numerous field trials, she was invariably, after leading the field, failed on her water retrieve.

It is really not very difficult to encourage any youngster, however hesitant, to enter water by first walking, in ordinary wellington boots, across a suitably shallow stretch of water encouraging the pup to follow. As a first introduction, preferably in the warmer summer months, something on these lines is sufficient. Even where the pup is clearly not in the least frightened several repetitions of this will do no harm. It is then advisable to don thigh boots and the trainer should gradually increase the depth of water through which he walks, so that the pup occasionally has to swim a few strokes. Meanwhile the pup should be watched carefully to see how it is accepting this new element and verbally encouraged. When it is obvious that it has grown quite accustomed to it, the next advance should be to choose a suitable place and cross in thigh waders, so that the pup has to swim a short distance. The exercise should be continued until the pup accepts swimming as a matter of course and can finally be sent across a river with the command 'Over' and a wave of the hand forward.

As may be seen from the foregoing there is now plenty to provide variety in the training. With two or more different walks each day and variations on the training included in them the pup should be stretched to the full all the time. Yet, despite the temptation to do so, it is important not to go ahead too fast. When a keen and intelligent pup seems to absorb its lessons almost as fast as they are taught it is easy to get carried away. It is only when suddenly the interest flags and the pup begins to make elementary mistakes that the trainer may suddenly realise, almost too late, that it has been pressed too hard and is showing the inevitable effects. This is a mistake that even an experienced trainer can very easily make with a very intelligent and forward pup.

Whenever a pup shows any signs of failure to understand a lesson, or unusual slowness, or plain rebellion, it is time to call a halt. Ease off the pressure at once and bring that particular lesson to an immediate end, even if it barely achieves more than a basic piece of obedience. Forget all the training for a while and then start again at something quite basic. Thereafter work back slowly to the point that had previously been reached and take it gently on from there once that stage has been reached again.

It has to be remembered that however disastrous a major mistake, or breakdown, in training may seem it is only another day in the context of the pup's lifetime. However bad it may seem at the time it is more than probable that the pup will have forgotten all about it in a week or so. Then a new approach may be begun from a different angle. It should be remembered that any gundog requires a long training, but those that are expected to master the pointer-retriever schedule require even longer. It is therefore essential to concentrate from the start on the initial training. Once this is mastered the rest of the training follows comparatively easily for it is only a matter of channelling instincts that are usually well developed.

It is, of course, true when training pointer-retrievers that where a pup proves very forward in either pointing, or retrieving, these instincts should be encouraged at the same time as the basic training. This is more with a view to ensuring that a good pup is not soured by any refusal to encourage its intrinsic gifts than by any real wish to start it on anything approaching real work before it is ready for it. It is unfortunately all too common to see pups with enormous natural working instincts and real potential, which have been encouraged by ignorant trainers to work before they have begun to absorb the all-essential initial training. The result is a spoiled dog which could well have been a field trial champion.

Where pups inherit very strong working instincts, of course, they may well be pointing strange sights, or even scents, before they are weaned, similarly they may start carrying small objects from the earliest age. It is important on the one hand to complete the initial training and at the same time not allow their natural instincts to become thwarted, or twisted, causing the pups themselves to become soured through not being allowed to fulfill these natural instincts. It is equally important not to start working a pup too soon, at an age when it should still just be enjoying life as a puppy, simply because it shows every sign of becoming a very able working dog. The answer is probably to take the pup on gently with initial retrieving, or pointing, at the same time as the initial training, but, once again, at all costs to avoid doing too much too soon.

OUTLINE OF POSSIBLE WEEKLY TRAINING SCHEDULE: SECONDARY STAGE:

First Week:

Acclimatise to car; get over car sickness: Train to accept place in basket when travelling: Introduce to town: Take into hotel: Walk on pavements: On usual lesson ground lay meat sandwich with mousetrap: Give warning 'No' as approached, but moved in and given fright: Start carrying gun during lessons: Walk out beside field of sheep: Interested in lambs, but firm 'No': Lessons varied twice daily, up to quarter of an hour: Double lessons at weekend.

Second Week:

Introduce to neighbouring house: Meet neighbouring dog and cat: Start to walk away, leaving pup sitting during training lesson; up to ten paces sufficient for week: Raising gun and swinging it when pup at distance, but no notice taken: Sandwich laid for pup but no attempt to pick and given warning 'No': Teach pup to get through fence to command 'Over': Introduce to hens; firm 'No', but sight point: Lessons as usual varied twice daily: Double lessons at weekend.

Third Week:

Gradually increasing distance at which pup can be left – up to thirty or forty paces: Dropping at once to whistle, hand signal and foot stamp, or command, when called to heel by signal, or whistle: Quite accustomed to gun and on suitably windy day assistant fires shot; successful introduction: Walk alongside field of cattle – frightened at first, but accustomed after second day: Lessons twice daily varied as usual and double at weekends.

Fourth Week:

Now walking up to hundred yards (91.4 m) away from pup and no attempt to move: Dropping readily on return and when out on own to drop whistle, signals, or command: Fully accustomed to gun and does not mind shot close at hand: Dropping to whistle at each shot; by end of week to shot alone: Long drop beside field of sheep successful: Lessons varied twice daily now up to twenty minutes and double at weekends.

Fifth Week:

Introduced to long check cord in walled garden: Kept sitting for five minutes first day and no attempt to move except as trainer vanished from sight, when checked with sharp tug on cord and firm 'No': Next day no attempt to move and wait of seven minutes: Introduced to rolling dummy with assistant; dropped with check cord after incipient move towards it; jerked off feet but unhurt: Lesson learned as no attempt to chase on second day; instead dropped to drop whistle well at distance: Dropping to shot and used to gun: Showing signs of pointing and carrying: Lessons varied each day and double at weekend.

Sixth Week:

Take out with neighbouring dog and drop to command and whistle despite no attention from other dog: Introduce to long shallow puddle up to gumboot level in places; enjoyed it: Next day introduce to river and crosses swimming a few paces; not frightened; natural water dog: By end of week swimming quite happily: Sight pointing now more common and carrying small toy around: Retrieving and pointing lessons shortly: Lessons varied and double at weekends.

Seventh and Eighth Weeks:

Continue long drop: Dropping to shot: Lengthen period of 'Stay': Teach crossing of fences and ditches: Increase water experience: Take long distance in car: Spend day in town: Walk through field of sheep on lead daily: Work alongside field of cattle: Use gun daily and drop to shot, whistle, signal and command at distance: Continue to vary lessons and prepare for more advanced training: At any sign of boredom, or disobedience, ease off training for day or more.

4 Initial Retrieving and Steadiness

It has already been indicated that some pups will have such ingrained instinct that they will be seen picking up and carrying objects around from the earliest days, even before they are weaned. Such indications of a strong natural instinct to retrieve should never in any way be discouraged. Rather than run the risk of the instinct possibly becoming warped and a deep-seated resistance to retrieving accidentally developing, it is best to channel it carefully from the start.

The object of the initial retrieving and steadiness training is primarily to teach the pup to pick up the dummy on command and retrieve it to the trainer. It must learn the meaning of the command 'Hie lost', or 'Fetch', whichever is chosen, to send the pup off on a retrieve. It must also learn the meaning of the command 'Dead', or 'Give', whichever is preferred, when delivering the dummy to the trainer and releasing it by opening its jaws. It must also learn the meaning of the command 'Mark', when the dummy is thrown into long grass, or other cover, to land out of sight. It might learn to sit obediently and mark the dummy's fall, only going to fetch it on command. It must learn to come directly back to the handler with the dummy, rather than circling wide of him, and it must learn to deliver directly to hand, rather than dropping it at a distance. It will have learned not only to sit unmoving when the dummy is thrown but to remain unmoving while the trainer goes forward to collect it. It should also have learned to mark the dummy and be able to go back to collect it from a distance when given the command 'Fetch mark'.

Even with a natural retriever it is unfortunately all too easy for a resistance to be caused accidentally during the formative puppyhood days. The result can be that when it finally comes to training the more adult animal it has already developed a deeply rooted objection to retrieving. This is frequently caused by some small incident such as the pup having retrieved a child's toy, then being chased, shouted at and having its prize indignantly snatched away from it. Alternatively the pup may often pick up and retrieve some unpleasant object such as a decaying dead rat which it brings triumphantly into the house and presents to its mistress, laying it proudly at her feet on the best carpet. Instead of receiving the praise it expects, this brings down a seemingly unwarranted scolding on its head. Such occurrences are unfortunately all too common and many professional trainers must have encountered stubborn refusals to retrieve caused by just such events in dogs which otherwise seemed to have every instinct well developed.

Where the pup is to be kept in the house, therefore, it is advisable that all members of the household should be trained to deal with such situations. When the pup retrieves something that is not desired the important point is to ensure that the retrieve itself is commended. Another article, such as a suitable sized dummy, may then be substituted for it and the pup allowed, even encouraged, to carry and deliver it instead. The unwanted article may then be shown to the pup with the warning prohibition 'No'.

One of the worst hazards facing the trainer at this stage, or indeed right up until the pup is fully trained, is the encounter with a very young, or crippled, bird, or rabbit suffering from myxomatosis. A fledgling, or cheeper, barely able to fly, or a sick, or injured, bird fluttering against a wire fence, or a half blind rabbit running uncertainly forward from tussock to tussock in the open are all very tempting objects to young and inexperienced pups with strongly developed hunting instincts. The trainer must always be on the alert for anything of this nature and whenever anything of this kind is seen the pup should as far as possible be brought into heel and checked beforehand with a firm 'No'.

If it is too late and the pup already has the bird, or animal, in its mouth, it is usually best to encourage it to complete the retrieve. Unfortunately this is not always possible. An old, crippled crow, which has damaged itself against telephone wires might well peck a pup quite severely and cause it to develop a serious resistance to retrieving. A baby rabbit, blinded by myxomatosis, struggling wildly in the pup's jaws, might well cause a tendency towards hard mouth. In such cases it might be best to give the prohibition 'No' and attempt to retrain the pup from further action, but a decision in such cases is not always easy.

If the worst has happened and the pup has thoroughly crunched some unfortunate cheeper, or baby rabbit, this is undesirable, to say the least, but it is not the end of everything. The best that can be done is to lead the pup away from the scene with as little fuss as possible and go on from there to distract its attention with something quite different. The important thing is to remain calm and avoid making much of the event thereby imprinting it on the pup's mind, which is the last thing that is required. The best policy on such occasions is to try to forget them as soon as possible and the chances are that no great harm will really have been done to the pup's progress. It may well, however, be wise to leave retrieving alone for a while until, with luck, the incident has been forgotten.

The type of toy, or plaything, provided for the pup is quite important. A ball, which can be squeezed in the mouth, is not desirable as it can result in the pup developing a habit of mouthing its retrieves and squeezing them, thus from an early age developing a tendency to be hard mouthed. For the same reason rubber squeaky toys and similar squeezable playthings are also inadvisable. A more suitable type of toy, as indicated earlier, might be a hard rubber bone, or a small rubber ring.

A length of rope, which may be pulled is not a particularly good plaything, since if it jams in an obstacle, such as a doorway the pup may then tug it and again start learning incipient bad habits. Especially when playing with another dog a toy which can easily be fought over, such as a length of rope, or a large rubber ring, each grabbing hold and having a tug of war, is much better avoided. This again may encourage the start of hard mouth.

Dummies for retrieving may be constructed in several ways.

A good old reliable standby is a dummy made from an old sock. Stuffed with old rags, or similar material, then sewn up these can be any size and weight desired. Their chief disadvantage is that they are not good in wet conditions since they soak up the damp. Using a stuffed rabbit skin is another common practice, but it is highly desirable that it is well cured. Even then it does not usually wear very well and may possibly on occasions lead to mouthing ground game at a later stage.

Probably best of all are those covered with really stout sail canvas. Good heavy duty canvas round a heavy duty rubber cylinder, stuffed with dried beans, or something similar, to provide suitable weight, can be made up to any desired size. These are both hard wearing and more or less proof against wet conditions. Several sizes and weights of dummy should be made, sewn with heavy duty twine and a sail needle, but no loose ends, or stitches, should be left which might snag a tooth. Properly made these should last several seasons.

The reason for suggesting several weights of dummy is that initially it is desirable to grade the size and weight of the dummy to the pup's growth. It is highly desirable to provide the pup with a dummy which is easy enough for it to pick up, but not so light that it is tempted to shake it triumphantly. Equally it should clearly not be too large for the pup to get its jaws round it, or so heavy that it is forced to drag it rather than carry it. While a pound or so may be heavy enough for a very young pup, a more mature dog will require at least three times as much. The trainer must clearly judge what is most suitable in each case and grade the dummy to the pup's size and development.

The dummies supplied with the normal dummy launcher may be all right once a pup has learned its initial retrieving, but are probably best left until it is suitably mature. Similarly it is desirable to leave any refinements, such as dummies equipped with bird's wings, or flaps, if the trainer feels them necessary, until the pup has learned to retrieve the normal dummy successfully. When that stage has been reached it may be felt that such devices are unnecessary and that it is better to go on to the real thing with a rather different approach.

Initial retrieving with a very young pup should only be carried out where it shows a persistent inclination to carry objects in its mouth. It is probably better in such cases to channel the retrieving instinct in the right direction from the start, rather than allow it to become accidentally thwarted, or perverted in some way. As indicated, it only requires some possibly unnoticed incident to cause the instinct to be blocked, diverted, or damaged so that a rooted resistance to retrieving is set up, or alternatively the retrieving itself is affected, by a refusal to bring to hand, persistent mouthing, or 'closing the suitcase' (i.e. hard mouth).

These very earliest retrieves of all may be conducted with the back to the kennel, or basket, taking advantage once again of the pup's natural instinct to run towards this refuge with a bone, or other prize. It is desirable to choose a favourite toy, or plaything, preferably one it has been noticed carrying, as the object of this very first retrieve. The trainer should be squatting, or kneeling, beside the pup close to the kennel, or basket. The object chosen as the one to be retrieved should then be thrown a short distance away with the command 'Hie Lost', or 'Fetch', whichever the trainer decides to use, and the pup should be encouraged with a wave of the hand to run forward to pick it up. If the pup is a natural retriever usually all will be easy and the pup will run forward to pick it up. It should then be encouraged to come to the trainer, who is now squatting, or kneeling, between it and the kennel, or basket. When it does so, the trainer may then intercept it, praising it highly and gently relieving it of its prize.

If the pup shows no inclination to let go of its toy, or plaything, its lips may be gently pressed against its teeth. As the pup then lets go the trainer should encourage it with the command 'Dead', or 'Give', whichever it has been decided to use. When the pup voluntarily relinquishes the toy, or plaything, it should be praised effusively and generally encouraged. The same, or a very similar, procedure may be adopted later when it is desired to teach a less forward pup initial retrieving. Even where it is feared that there might be difficulty in getting the pup to pick up and carry this procedure should still be successful and is certainly worth trying at the start, although it is, of course, essential to choose some object which the pup has been seen to carry previously.

Once these absolute basic preliminaries to retrieving have been overcome and the pup will run to pick up a dummy thrown in the open and retrieve it to hand, the first hurdle is over. It should be added that in most cases, when the pup has been introduced to the idea of retrieving at the right moment, only one such lesson is likely to be required. With an intelligent pup properly handled the chances are high that after this very first performance it will require no further lesson. It will at once understand what is required and will be happy to fetch the dummy to hand. Even if the lesson has not gone perfectly the object is to get the pup to run forward and pick up the dummy and carry it. If that has been achieved the main point has been made.

It may be that the pup will run forward eagerly, pounce on the dummy and shake it, standing staring challengingly at the trainer, eager to return to its kennel, or basket, but baulked by the sight of the trainer in the way. In such a case the trainer should turn away towards the kennel, or basket, and encourage the pup verbally. The chances are that the pup will then come and it should, of course, be highly praised when it does so. This cannot be over emphasized, at any stage in the training, but especially initially, for when a pup receives little or no praise it soon becomes discouraged and disobedient.

If there is any problem about the pup bringing the object to be retrieved directly to the trainer, the answer is to ensure that circumstances are such that it has no choice. If, for example, it circles round to reach its kennel, or basket, the trainer should stand in a narrow passageway so that the pup has to come to him direct. A corridor in a house is ideal for the purpose, but in the open a gateway, or doorway, or similar opening, is just as effective. The pup cannot then slip past the trainer waiting to intercept it.

If this initial retrieving training is left until the pup is more mature, so much the better, for by then its basic training should have reached the stage where this can be used to encourage it more readily to come to the trainer. The principle, however, remains perfectly sound and rather than wait until the rest of the initial training has progressed to a suitable stage it is usually worthwhile starting the pup on this initial retrieving whenever it shows signs of wishing to pick up objects and carry them around.

It is always better to channel instinct whenever it appears, rather than allow it a chance to become blocked, or perverted, in some way. If, in practice, the pup shows no signs of retrieving, or any interest in doing so, this aspect of training can happily be left until the initial obedience training is complete and, for that matter, until the pup is pointing, if that is the instinct which first asserts itself.

Having surmounted the first hurdle of encouraging the pup to pick up and carry back to the trainer, without, it is to be hoped, much difficulty, the next stage is to carry out the early retrieves in the open. For this purpose a tussocky, grassy area, which is secluded and free from the danger of any interruptions is desirable. Although by this time the pup may have been receiving its initial training with various distractions around, sometimes with them even being positively encouraged, it is important with these early retrieving lessons especially to avoid the danger of interruptions which could have very adverse effects. Any piece of land where there may be strangers passing without warning, or where stray dogs might appear, such as a park, or common, simply will not do at this stage. Any interruption of this sort in these early lessons could well distract the pup's intention at a crucial point and cause a resistance to retrieving to develop in the pup's mind.

In addition to outside distractions it is highly desirable that the ground itself should not have too many scents, or game, such as rabbits, present, which could be very distracting to say the least. A brace of partridges rising under the pup's nose, or a moorhen in boggy ground, could be just the sort of distraction it least requires when being sent out on its early retrieves. Anything in the way of dead carcases, of rats, or birds, or other similar smelly objects, are also best removed beforehand, although this is sometimes easier said than done and the trainer should never be surprised by what the pup may retrieve accidentally when sent forward in these early lessons. Ancient corpses of animals, or birds, are commonplace, but an abandoned ham sandwich in a cellophane wrapping, a child's lost toy, and even a half bottle of whisky filled with stale milk, left over from a picnic, are amongst the objects which I have personally had retrieved to me on these occasions.

On the very first of these retrieves in the open it is preferable that the pup is able to see the dummy thrown and also to watch it fall in full view. If there is any conceivable doubt about the pup retrieving, it should not be restrained on this very first retrieve in the open, but should be encouraged to run forward with a wave of the hand and the command. The trainer should then squat to encourage it to retrieve to hand. Thereafter the dummy may be thrown so that the pup can see it fall in long grass and mark it, but it should be restrained by the trainer for a moment or two, until the command is given with a wave of the hand forward. The trainer should then squat again to encourage the pup to retrieve to hand direct. The trainer must also, of course, praise the pup warmly while relieving it gently of the dummy with the appropriate command.

It is essential, of course, in these early retrieves to prepare matters as far as possible to ensure success beforehand. Thus it is preferable, as already stressed, to ensure that there will be no distractions, either on the ground itself, or as far as possible from outside. Nor should the pup ever be given anything in the way of retrieves which might be beyond its powers. The dummy should be graded specifically to the pup's size and ability. It should not be thrown more than a few yards and it should only be thrown upwind, so that even if the pup fails to mark it properly in the long grass there should be little or no difficulty in finding it at once. The trainer should also make certain of standing in a gateway, or narrow opening, so that the pup cannot circle round, but has to bring the dummy directly to hand. If all these points have been covered in advance these early and very important retrieves should be carried out successfully without any difficulty.

After the first few retrieves have been successful and the pup has learned to sit while watching the dummy being thrown and marking its fall in long grass, then retrieving it, the time has come to vary the lesson. The next stage is comparatively simple but since it is combined with the initial training some care should be taken that the pup has attained the required standards in this aspect of training and that the two are not in any way conflicting. Initially the dummy may be thrown and the pup made to sit while the handler walks forward and picks up the dummy, bringing it back to where the pup remains sitting. The pup will thus have the lesson that it must not move when told to sit reinforced and it will also learn that it may not always be sent to retrieve when the dummy is thrown. Two useful lessons can thus each be used to enforce the other.

When the first few simple retrieves have been successful and the trainer is certain that the pup has learned to mark the dummy falling in long grass, another advance is to throw the dummy where it will certainly be marked quite easily. The command 'Mark' should then be given and after repeating this command once more the pup should be led away, preferably on the lead to avoid any danger of running back, although if the initial training has reached a sufficient standard simply at heel. Some ten or fifteen paces away the trainer should halt and turn round, with the pup sitting at heel, then give a forward wave and the command 'Fetch mark'. If the progression has been kept well within the pup's abilities it should have no bother in at once finding and retrieving the dummy as before. It should, of course, be highly praised and thereafter the distances may be gradually increased.

As in the very first instance it is important in all these early retrieves to make use of the wind by ensuring that the pup is working into the wind so that the scent of the dummy is clearly wafted towards it. This will ensure that the pup has little or no trouble in these early stages and will also give it considerable confidence. This should also serve to show the trainer how well developed the pup's powers of scenting are at this stage and in general it is usually surprising how far advanced they are from a very early age.

As the pup progresses it may soon be possible to start sending it down wind. More difficult retrieving of this nature should, however, be reserved for the time when the pup has proved itself fully capable of retrieving into the wind and will fetch the dummy to hand without fail. It should also be able to retrieve a mark at a considerable distance into the wind before starting on downwind retrieves. By this time, to some extent at least, the pup should also have learned the meaning and use of hand signals as the trainer directs it forward onto the dummy. Only then should the downwind retrieves be started.

There are a number of resistances the trainer may encounter during these early retrieving lessons and as far as possible they will be dealt with individually. The first, of course, is a refusal to pick up the dummy at all, even though the very first retrieves of all went well enough. If this is the case these preliminary lessons are probably best left until more keeness to carry is apparent. As has been stressed it is always better to channel instinct once it has been evinced, rather than try to force the pup on at too early a stage. A total refusal to pick up the dummy at this stage probably indicates that the pup is not yet ready for the lessons and the trainer should just continue to concentrate on the initial training. There will be plenty of time later to introduce retrieving when the pup shows it is ready for it.

Even where the pup shows it is keen to pick up and retrieve the dummy there are still a number of resistances which are liable to arise in the early stages. For example it is quite common for the pup to perform perfectly in the first instance and for the first few retrieves, then for it to start behaving indifferently. A common example is a seeming inability to find the dummy. Although the pup may have previously marked the dummy perfectly and shown that it has a good nose by retrieving it even in long grass, it will start to run past it without looking at it. This blatant ignoring of the dummy is, of course, merely the pup's way of indicating that it is tired of the lesson. The trainer has almost certainly been overdoing it and the pup is plainly bored and showing the fact in the only way it can. The answer is to lay off this particular aspect of training for a week or more and then repeat the lesson much less often with frequent variations to keep the pup's interest from flagging.

It is extremely easy for the keen amateur trainer, eager to watch his pup developing fast, to over estimate its powers and abilities. In his, or her, own keeness to get on with the training it is very easy for such a trainer to press a pup too hard. This is a very common failing with a novice trainer and one that should be avoided as far as possible since it inevitably leads to setbacks which can become serious. A trainer should always be on the lookout for signs that a young pup is being pushed beyond its capabilities and being asked to do too much.

One of the commonest resistances at this stage is a refusal to retrieve to hand. This may be presaged by the pup picking up the dummy, pouncing on it, playing with it, tossing it in the air, mouthing it, or even shaking it violently, before finally coming to the trainer. Alternatively it may come towards the trainer, but stop just out of reach and drop the dummy, spreading its forepaws, as if for a game. Or again it may turn away from the trainer, circling round, as if suggesting it should be chased. All these are examples of typical immature puppy behaviour, showing a desire to play, rather than taking the lessons seriously. In every such case they are an indication that the pup is probably still too young for the lessons and a rest is desirable. In such cases it is best to revert for a period to simple initial training and allow the pup plenty of time for play.

The trainer should always watch the pup carefully for any such signs of incipient boredom. If he sees any of them the best course is to bring that lesson promptly to a close and lay off the training for a short period until the pup is interested once again. The period of rest, it may be added, should depend to some extent on the degree of resistance shown by the pup. The aim, as far as possible, is never to give the pup reason to feel that it has found a successful method of imposing its will on the trainer. If the lessons are continued with such reactions they will only go from bad to worse.

A very similar resistance is for the pup to start dropping the dummy at the trainer's feet, rather than giving it to hand. This may have been caused by pressing the pup's lips too hard against its teeth to encourage it to release the dummy. Or it may be caused by fear of the trainer's height. In such cases it is not a good idea to pick the dummy up, or in any way scold the pup. It is better to take several paces backwards then crouch down and encourage the pup verbally to pick up the dummy again and as it approaches turn away encouraging it verbally all the while so that it is forced to walk alongside the trainer at heel. The pup will then soon appreciate that it is only expected to release the dummy when given the command to do so.

If on the other hand the pup shows signs of refusing to come to the trainer, on no account must he, or she, advance towards the pup. This will merely encourage it to turn and run off, with or without the dummy, hoping to be chased. In such circumstances the trainer should instead turn away from the pup and encourage it to follow by running in the opposite direction. The instinct to chase is very nearly invariably overpowering and the pup will almost certainly run after the trainer, usually with the dummy in its mouth.

Once the pup is close to the trainer, there are several alternative courses of action open. The trainer may bend down, patting the knee, encouraging the pup to come, coaxing it verbally at the same time, then squatting to accept the dummy and praising it for delivering. Alternatively the trainer may give the command 'Sit' and bend down to accept the dummy, if the pup is still holding it. In any event, whether the pup retrieves the dummy, or has left it lying, the important thing is to end the lesson with some action successfully performed to command. For instance, praising the pup for coming to heel, dropping to command, or whatever the trainer has succeeded eventually in enforcing. Thereafter return home with the pup at heel on the lead and start afresh with initial training on the next outing, before starting retrieving lessons again.

Where a pup shows no apparent natural instinct to retrieve at all, the question the novice trainer will naturally be asking is when the retrieving training should start. Fortunately this is not a question which normally arises as total lack of interest in retrieving is uncommon. It is preferable to start when the pup starts to show a natural inclination to carry, but, as noted, this may have been accidentally stifled earlier by some seemingly insignificant incident quite unknown to the trainer. However, when the pup is from nine months to a year old, although still a youngster, with plenty of growth to come, it should be ready for the initial retrieving and steadiness training.

The trainer may in any event prefer to start with pointing training. There are certainly those who advocate this in any event and it may be that the pup naturally excels in this direction, rather than in retrieving. By this time, however, it should

have been evincing some interest in retrieving. Total refusal
even to pick up and carry something at this stage is likely to be
difficult to overcome and the resistance has probably been
formed as a result of some incident in puppyhood.

The important thing, as with the younger pup, is always first
to find some object which the youngster is prepared to carry.
Initially this may have to be a bone, or plaything. It is very rare
for any breed of dog, especially gundogs, to show a total refusal
to carry anything in its mouth, whatever mistakes may have
been made in its upbringing. The same basic principle of getting
between the youngster and its kennel, or basket, applies as
described earlier. Whatever the object chosen to be retrieved
should then be thrown and the youngster made much of when it
is intercepted.

Where the trainer does encounter a total refusal to pick up
and carry, the use of jealousy may, of course, prove a potent
means of persuasion. This is always a powerful weapon in the
trainer's armoury, although it should be used with care. At any
point during the training a mature, trained gundog may be used
to set the youngster an example, which is often immediately
copied. If the trainer has several dogs in the kennels the example
of another youngster can also often be enough to set the
recalcitrant pup on the right lines. When it comes to retrieving
this is very much the case. Merely demonstrating another
inmate of the kennel fetching the dummy may be enough to set
an example the pup is prepared to emulate. Alternatively a
friend's trained gundog brought in for the purpose may perform
the same service.

If the recalcitrant youngster is held on the lead while the
dummy is thrown for the other dog to retrieve the probability is
that a certain natural jealousy will be aroused. This natural
reaction should be encouraged by effusively praising the other
dog. If the other dog is encouraged to carry the dummy at heel
and is highly praised while doing so the problem youngster will
probably be unable to resist straining forward to sieze it. The
trainer should, of course, be watching the youngster's reactions
carefully. Any such reaction indicating interest, however slight,
means the psychological moment has probably arrived to throw

the dummy for it to fetch and see whether the lesson has gone home.

In many cases this will prove to be enough and the lesson will be performed, if not perfectly, at least in part. The initial resistance should have been overcome and it should then simply be a question of taking the lessons on from there. Once the dummy has actually been picked up and carried, however indifferently, the first all-important progress has been made. The major breakthrough is when the youngster starts to show interest and this applies to all aspects of training.

A certain amount, of course, must depend on the novice trainer's views on what constitutes picking up and carrying, or for that matter retrieving. The doctor, mentioned earlier (p. 19), who appeared to be a keen shooting man and to whom I had sold a pup, rang me up with a series of complaints after two or three months. Prominent amongst these was the fact that the youngster would not retrieve. When pressed he indicated that it would not even pick up and carry.

Knowing that the sire and dam were both excellent natural retrievers I was surprised to hear this and agreed to visit him. When I arrived he opened the door and the pup, looking well cared for admittedly, came out behind him, apparently pleased to see me. Before greeting the doctor I gave the pup my cap and he circled round with it in his jaws and very happily gave it up to hand when I called him.

'It doesn't look to me as if there's any problem about his retrieving!' I said, rather pointedly.

The doctor mumbled that he was surprised by the youngster's action, but I hardly listened to his reply for my eye had fallen on an amazing pile of scrubbing brushes, plastic buckets, dish towels, sponges and similar washing materials which made a heap about three foot high on his front lawn. I enquired what on earth they were doing there and he explained that the pup had a habit of wandering down to the row of nearby council houses where it picked up anything lying around and brought it back to the house. It seemed everyone was accustomed to this and merely came to collect whatever they had lost. It was obvious, of course, that I had sold the pup to a remarkably bad home, but after some discussion he agreed on his part that he would build the dog a kennel with a decent run, if I took it back to train. It was, of course, very stupid of me, but I was trying to do my best for the dog. The road to hell is truly paved with good intentions.

Such determined refusal to admit to retrieving ability in a pup is unusual to say the least, but genuine cases of refusal to retrieve do occur and can be difficult to cure. With absolutely determined cases of refusal to pick up the dummy in a mature youngster of a year or more, it may be necessary to enlist an assistant to hold the youngster firmly on the lead. The dummy may then be placed gently in the youngster's jaws and held firmly in place. If the youngster struggles, or tries to spit it out, the trainer must firmly but gently prevent it. The pup should at the same time be praised verbally and stroked gently with one hand, while the other holds the dummy in place. After a few moment's unavailing struggle the youngster will probably become resigned and gradually its tail should start to wave. Once this happens the trainer may be sure that with a little patience the youngster will soon be carrying the dummy without any trouble and the retrieving training can then be started. Should the youngster win this battle of wills, of course, then it has proved conclusively that it will not retrieve at least for that trainer.

With mature dogs of around two years or more, where refusal to retrieve is due to stubborness, rather than fright, it may as a last resort, be necessary to use a minimal degree of force. This is not advocated except in the case of advanced refusal with a mature dog, when all other efforts, such as those described above, have failed. Forced retrieving is quite commonly used on the continent and in North America, but despite what its advocates claim, it is never as satisfactory as channelling the natural instincts in the right direction. This is dealt with fully in the chapter on training the mature dog and it should never be considered in relation to a pup, or immature youngster. Wherever the instinct is still apparent it is merely up to the trainer to encourage it on the right lines.

POSSIBLE WEEKLY TRAINING SCHEDULE:
INITIAL RETRIEVING:

First Week:

Early retrieve with plaything, which the pup has been consistently carrying: Thrown from near basket to doorway; command 'Fetch' given; intercepted on way back and relieved of plaything with command 'Give': Very slight pressure required on lips against teeth: Next day dummy thrown into edge of short grass with puppy sitting at heel, waved forward at once with command 'Fetch'; dummy brought to hand in gateway; semi-intercept: By end of week retrieving dummy from edge of long grass to hand: Sitting until waved forward and given command.

Second Week:

First three days merely made to sit and retrieve when dummy thrown into long grass: Command 'Mark' given when thrown: Pup kept at heel; dummy upwind in edge of grass, but hidden from view: Waved forward to retrieve with command 'Fetch mark'; coming back to gateway and intercepted, trainer crouching, giving up dummy to command 'Give': Change of scene each time but essentials the same: Second three days, alternate retrieve with trainer fetching dummy and pup remaining at 'Sit'. At end of week after command 'Mark' moved pup two or three paces each time: Retrieves still all upwind.

Third Week:

Alternating between straight retrieves, trainer picking up dummy and moving increasing distance with pup at heel after command 'Mark': Progress to twenty or thirty paces after command 'Mark' before pup sent to retrieve: Retrieves still all upwind and not thrown too far into long grass: Each time ground different to some degree, but all comparatively simple; hand signals increasingly used: At weekend try first down wind retrieves; still easy.

Fourth Week:

Alternating between dummy thrown up wind and down wind; retrieves by trainer and by pup: Distance of mark now up to fifty paces, but still only upwind to ensure success: Retrieves gradually being made a little harder upwind; care being taken downwind; assisting with hand signals and whistle and pup responding; trainer still crouching, but probably not necessary.

Fifth and Sixth Weeks:

Continue to provide variety of retrieves upwind and down: Marks now made from distance but also retrieving after returning to original position from some distance: Pup marking very accurately; retrieving to hand; giving up dummy immediately on command 'Give': Moving fast to retrieve and on return to trainer; retrieves becoming gradually more difficult, but now ready to go on to more advanced retrieving.

5 Advanced Retrieving and Steadiness

In the initial retrieving and steadiness lessons the pup has learned to respond to the command 'Hie lost', or 'Fetch', and to 'Dead', or 'Give', whichever has been chosen, as well as to the command 'Mark'. It has learned to retrieve a dummy directly to hand and deliver it on command. It has learned to sit at heel unmoving while the dummy is thrown into long grass and to mark its fall. The pup will remain without moving until given the appropriate command and a forward wave of the arm. When sent to fetch the dummy it is beginning to respond to hand signals. It will remain sitting while the trainer goes forward to fetch the dummy. It has also been taught to go back to fetch the dummy from a distance when it has once been marked. The time has now come to introduce it to more advanced retrieving in preparation for work in the field.

The object of the advanced retrieving and steadiness training is to bring the pup to the stage where it is ready to meet any problem it is likely to encounter in the field. To start with it must have not merely one dummy, but two, thrown to retrieve, with the commands 'Mark one' and 'Mark two'. This at once allows for much greater variation in the training. Thereafter the gun may also be introduced, with, if desired, a dummy launcher. The next point is to introduce distractions, such as another dummy thrown while the pup is retrieving, or the rolling dummy. This should be followed by retrieves from and across water and from cover. From this stage onwards, downwind retrieves and unseen retrieves, or retrieves over obstacles, may be increasingly introduced. Finally the youngster should be introduced to dead game and then to laid trails, of increasing difficulty, on dead birds. The youngster should then be ready for work in the field.

With the start of the advanced retrieving and steadiness training the trainer's options are very considerably widened yet again. To begin with the dummy retrieving may now take place in areas where disturbances are likely to be encountered, or where distractions may appear on hand. People passing nearby, or stock in fields alongside, are the sort of distraction with which the pup should be expected to cope in the first instance. The presence of another dog, or dogs, as well as other handlers, as at a training class, are extremely good preparation for retrieving in the field at a later date. It is still advisable, however, to try to avoid the disturbing scents of live game as much as possible until the pup is fully aware of their meaning. The presence of ground game, especially, is on the whole better avoided until the trainer has attained a high standard of initial obedience training.

The first really big advance for the pup as regards the new retrieving regime is the throwing not just of one dummy only, but two, one after the other, in opposite directions. As each dummy is thrown the trainer should, as it were, name it, by giving the command 'Mark one' for the first and 'Mark two' for the second. The next stage is to direct the pup with a definite wave of the hand and the arm and the command 'Fetch', or 'Hie lost', adding 'Mark one', or 'Mark two', depending on which has been chosen for the first retrieve. It is worth making the point that for the first few occasions at least the dummies should be thrown so that, although almost at right angles to each other, both are slightly forward of the trainer standing facing into the wind, thus making each retrieve as simple as possible. It is still desirable at this stage, as throughout the pup's early training at least, to ensure that it is successful and thus, by avoiding any failures, build up its confidence in its own abilities.

When the pup has retrieved the first dummy, in response to the command, prefaced with the addition of 'Mark one' and a clear wave of the hand pointing in the appropriate direction, the decision as to whether the second should be retrieved is up to the trainer. It may be that once the first has been retrieved the trainer decides that the second is best retrieved by hand, thus once again teaching the pup restraint. A certain amount must depend on how well the pup performs the first retrieve. If it is showing signs of exuberance a slight check, such as making it sit while the trainer fetches the second dummy, may be just what is required. On the other hand it may be that after receiving the first dummy to hand the trainer decides to send the pup for the second also, prefacing the command to fetch with the addition of 'Mark two' and a wave of the hand pointing clearly in the required direction.

Another variation on the same situation, with two dummies marked, might be for the trainer to send the pup to retrieve the first, then lead it some distance away before sending it to retrieve the second. Alternatively the trainer might fetch the first and send the pup for the second, or else take it some distance away before doing so. From this stage onwards, as may be appreciated, the number of alternatives open on each occasion is steadily increasing, which makes for more varied training and increases the interest for the trainer as well as for the pup. Not only is the interest growing for both trainer and pup, but the training is becoming much closer to the real thing. Having been thoroughly grounded in basic obedience in the initial training, the pup is now learning to prepare for every aspect of its work as a pointer-retriever in the field.

At this stage the trainer may start carrying a gun as well as throwing dummies. Alternatively it is useful while carrying a gun to have an assistant in attendance equipped with a gun and the dummies or a dummy launcher. While the trainer is walking with the pup at heel, or out in front, the gun may be fired and a dummy thrown. The pup should drop to the sound of the shot, but should also have marked the fall of the dummy and may then be sent to fetch it. The pup must now become accustomed to retrieving to the trainer's spare hand while the gun is being held under the other arm.

If a dummy launcher is used at this point, the pup should, of course, drop to the sound of the dummy launcher being fired, as to shot. It is essential, however, to make sure that it is not fired as the pup is either going to or coming back from a retrieve. At this stage no shot should be fired while the pup is retrieving as this may only confuse it and the one thing to be avoided at any time is causing confusion in the youngster's mind. It is essential that each command, or lesson, should lead smoothly on to another with as far as possible no conflict.

It is probably a good plan therefore to introduce the rolling dummy again at this stage by way of distraction. This should be thrown to one side of the pup just when it has almost completed a comparatively simple retrieve. As indicated, an assistant is useful for this, but by choosing suitable ground the trainer should be able to bowl the dummy at speed, leaping and bounding erratically, past the pup. If it has been thoroughly grounded in its initial obedience training the pup should start to drop, or at the very least hesitate. The trainer should encourage verbally the pup to continue the retrieve and duly praise it when it does so. The next obvious move is to wait once more until the pup has almost completed a simple retrieve and then for the trainer, or assistant, to throw another dummy in full view. Again the pup must be encouraged verbally to continue the retrieve and praised when it does so. It should thus shortly come to appreciate that, once started, a retrieve must be completed regardless of distractions.

There are now several options open to the trainer, and it is probably as well to leave the matter of double retrieves and distractions alone for the moment in order to provide variety for the pup. The next logical progression in this line, however, is for two dummies to be thrown and then to follow this with not one but two distractions. The rolling dummy may be thrown to one side and another dummy thrown to the other as the pup returns with the retrieve that has been chosen. This is emphasising the point that the pup must not leave a retrieve once started for there are few things more irritating in the field than the half trained dog which starts a retrieve and then puts it down in order to fetch another bird which has fallen nearby. With an excitable young dog this can result in several retrieves half completed and eventually no bird to hand.

At some point in the training, when the trainer feels it is suitable, the final distraction of another shot fired as the pup is retrieving may also be introduced. On the first occasion this is probably best introduced with the addition of a thrown dummy when the pup is fairly close at hand after a simple retrieve. By this time the pup should have appreciated that once started on a retrieve nothing must prevent it finishing the task, but again verbal encouragement should be given at the appropriate moment and the pup duly praised when the retrieve is completed. The final progression in this particular aspect of retrieving is for several dummies to be thrown and the pup to be directed to each in turn, as required, with distractions including shots and further dummies, as desired. The pup can thus be prepared for picking up prior to the end of a drive, while birds are still falling. Although this may seldom be required it can be a considerable advantage sometimes when picking up to be able to send a dog onto a particular runner which might otherwise be lost to the bag. For this, such training is ideal and it is all good training in steadiness.

By this time the retrieves will be taking place in country where there may well be distractions of all sorts and it is as well that the pup should be trained to withstand them. Inevitably the pup will from time to time encounter scents of game, if not the real thing itself. Any such occasions when, for instance, a brace of partridges are flushed, or a rabbit, or hare, accidentally encountered, the opportunity should be taken to make the pup drop at once to the flush of the game.

The stage has now been reached where the pup may start retrieving from, or across, water. Initially the dummy may be thrown to land in the water with a resounding splash and the pup may then be sent to retrieve it. As the pup has already been accustomed to entering water there should be no difficulty about the dummy being fetched, although the pup should be checked if it shows any tendency to put the dummy down and shake itself after coming out of the water. When the dummy is retrieved to hand the pup should duly be praised and allowed to shake itself as much as it likes.

After the straightforward retrieve from water it may be desired to extend the lesson by throwing two dummies into the water and accustoming the pup to retrieving them in turn. Since this will accustom the pup to working to hand signals in the water it is a useful advance. From there it is a small step to retrieving from across water. Here, initially, the pup may be allowed to see the dummy thrown to land on the opposite bank and be encouraged to cross the water with the command 'Over'. Once again on successfully accomplishing the retrieve the pup should be praised. Thereafter there may be one retrieve from water and one from across water, both being thrown in full view of the pup and each being taken in turn as required.

In addition to the water retrieve the time has now come to introduce the pup to retrieving from cover. Initially it is best to keep this comparatively simple, by using cover, which while reasonably thick is not likely to discourage the pup. Thus reeds, or well grown grass, or similar thick but comparatively harmless cover should be sufficient in the first instance. Once the pup has become accustomed to burrowing into the cover to retrieve the dummy rather more difficult cover may be tried. Prickly brambles, gorse, thorny cover and nettle grown ground are all likely to test the youngster considerably and initially it is advisable not to throw the dummy too far into difficult ground of this nature in order not to discourage the pup.

If the pup shows signs of not facing more difficult thick cover, such as gorse and brambles, there is no need to be unduly discouraged. Later on when it comes to the real thing it is likely to be a different story. In any event the youngster should never be taxed beyond its powers and thus discouraged. The aim of all training should be to encourage the youngster and inspire it with confidence in itself and in its trainer. As already clearly shown, it is better to progress in small stages rather than try to take on too much at once and fail.

The time should certainly now have been reached, however, when the pup can go onto downwind retrieves. Although to start with these should be thrown so that the pup may mark them easily and be in comparatively simple ground, to ensure that no mistake is made, they can soon be made more difficult. Once the pup is accustomed to working downwind it makes the retrieving more interesting and again the trainer's options are increased. It is now possible to vary the training so that one dummy is thrown downwind and another upwind, or the pup led upwind of a marked retrieve so that it has to retrieve downwind, hence encouraging it to mark accurately.

With the wide variety of options now available to the trainer there should be no excuse for allowing the pup to become in any way bored. The initial training in obedience will now be more or less complete, but will still be a part of the training day. Combining it with the advanced retrieving should ensure that there is little or no trouble with awkward reactions, or resistances, although, inevitably, with each pup some points are likely to go better than with others. There may be difficulties with some aspect such as the water retrieve, or retrieving from cover, but, as with every other stage of training, the answer is simply to approach matters slowly and build up confidence by degrees.

It should now be possible while walking out with the pup to throw a dummy to one side with the command 'Mark'. Several hundred yards further on the command 'Fetch, mark' should be all that is required. The youngster, accustomed to retrieves which have been steadily lengthened, should find this no problem. In this way, quite apart from anything else, it is possible to give the dog considerable exercise, building up its fitness for its work in the field in due course.

It is important also that the command 'Over' should be clearly taught at this stage. The early retrieves over a wall or fence, obviously should not be difficult. Sitting the dog at heel facing a low wall, or simple wire fence, it is only necessary to throw the dummy so that it falls in long grass the far side of the obstacle. The trainer should, however, be able to see exactly where it falls and thus be able to watch the youngster after it has crossed the obstacle on the command 'Fetch, over' and a wave of the arm pointing in the required direction. The dog should be encouraged verbally to make the retrieve and when it approaches the obstacle again should once more be given the command 'Over', prior to bringing the dummy to hand.

The next obvious stage in the training schedule is the introduction of unseen retrieves. Here, for the first time, the youngster is faced with being sent off to find a dummy which it has not seen thrown. Prior to going out with the pup the trainer should have laid the dummy in position, having taken the precaution of leaving a stick in the ground to act as a marker near the dummy and another at the point from which it is intended to send the pup, for it is often quite simple to mislay the dummy unless this precaution is taken. The pup should then be led out in the normal manner and when the first marker has been reached the gun may be fired in the direction of the dummy and the command and signal given to retrieve. Since the first retrieve of this nature should be upwind the pup should have little trouble in finding it and bringing it to hand, but thereafter the retrieves should be progressively more difficult.

It should not be very long before more than one dummy can be laid out prior to the lesson, with markers in position for the trainer's benefit, and the pup duly directed to them in the course of the lesson without any shot being fired. It should soon, in practice, be possible to send the pup for unseen retrieves across water, or over obstacles, such as fences, or walls, with the command to retrieve and the command 'Over' adding the encouragement 'On', in addition to the hand signals. In due course the pup should be retrieving dummies in unseen retrieves at considerable distances with the aid of whistles and hand signals. Eventually the pup should be retrieving dummies laid out in this manner as unseen retrieves downwind, responding simply to the command to retrieve and the whistles and directing waves of the hand.

At this stage there are those who argue that it is advisable to prepare the youngster to deal with retrieving game birds by using dummies which have pheasant wings sewn on to them, or else have flaps of canvas hanging from them to simulate wings. In that this is a form of gradual progression towards the real thing it seems to me there is no real objection to it. On the other hand it really does not seem very necessary. Indeed it could be that the pheasant wings, smelling somewhat of corruption, or else of formaldehyde, might have a bad effect, causing the youngster to shake, or mouth, the dummy, or even refuse to pick it up altogether.

The time has certainly come when it is advisable to introduce the youngster to something approaching the real thing. This may be done in several ways. A method advocated by some is to enclose a recently killed pigeon inside a tube formed from the leg of a pair of nylon tights. These should, of course, have been thoroughly washed before use to remove any scent of their previous owner affecting the issue. Securely tied at each end this can make a neat tight bundle, smelling distinctly of dead bird, but not providing a mouthful of feathers when picked up by the youngster.

One of the snags with this idea is that when the youngster approaches this first retrieve smelling of blood and death it is almost certain to have misgivings. It will almost certainly pick it up with considerable care. The chances are that the bundle will be picked up by one of the knots at each end and carried to the handler triumphantly, dangling delicately from the teeth. This is not exactly the lesson it has been aimed at teaching the pup, for the pup is not likely to find any convenient nylon knots dangling from dead game. In practice this method can, therefore, have disadvantages, although in theory it is quite a sound idea.

Probably one of the soundest ways to introduce the youngster to retrieving dead game is to start with a recently killed old bird, preferably an old partridge, or an old cock pheasant, or a mallard. The disadvantage of both pigeons and grouse is that they tend to have too many loose feathers which are liable to adhere to a youngster's mouth and cause them a certain discomfort. This can lead to mouthing, to refusal to retrieve, or similar resistances.

Whatever bird is chosen should have been cleanly killed. There should be as little blood as possible and, of course, no damage such as broken ribs, or wings, possibly with broken bones sticking out, which could jab the youngster's mouth. On the whole it is desirable to let the game grow cold, but to ensure that it is tucked into a neat and easily retrievable bundle. With the head tucked under a wing and the legs into the body a broad rubber band should be stretched round the bird holding it into a compact shape for retrieving.

Without the youngster being aware of it the bird should then be placed upwind. When a suitable point has been reached downwind, the pup may then be sent off with a wave of the hand in the direction of the planted bird. It will almost certainly find it at once, but since this is a strange new scent the pup will probably approach it with care and it may well pause in a sight point before picking it. At this stage it should be encouraged verbally by the trainer to help it over this natural reaction of distaste. As soon as it has picked the bird up it should again be encouraged verbally to return with it to hand. Should it show any signs of mouthing, or intention of putting the bird down the trainer should again encourage it verbally, or use the prohibition 'No', to ensure it is brought to hand. With the background training it has had the likelihood is that the pup will bring it to hand, even if this first retrieve is not necessarily a model of its kind.

Sometimes the youngster will show considerable antipathy to the smell of blood and will develop a tendency to mouth the game, even insisting on putting it down at intervals, despite verbal encouragement, or prohibition, from the trainer. In such circumstances it may be advisable to switch to water retrieves. For these a shot mallard should be used, neatly bound with a broad rubber band as indicated. Thrown into the water, or placed there beforehand, as the trainer prefers, the youngster should then be sent to retrieve the bird.

The duck being a close-feathered bird, there is little chance of feathers adhering to the dog's mouth, which is often a cause of mouthing and in the water anyway the youngster has little choice. The bird will almost certainly be retrieved well until the pup starts to leave the water. To avoid any difficulty at this point the trainer should be ready and waiting to take the bird. The pup should then, be praised and patted. After the first two or three retrieves of this kind the initial repugnance will probably be overcome and a land retrieve on suitably-bound dead game will most likely prove successful.

Sometimes the youngster may show an antipathy to retrieving dead feathered game including mallard, but can be persuaded to show a greater interest by starting it on ground game. A suitable old rabbit cleanly shot and neatly laid on its stomach, thus presenting a similar appearance to a dummy, may be put out for the youngster. When the pup is sent to retrieve, the trainer should watch its reactions carefully. Again there is likely to be a somewhat careful inspection, but the chances are that a sensitive pup will more willingly retrieve ground game to hand. Once again its is desirable to encourage it verbally while it is hesitating and as it brings the game to hand. It usually only requires a few successful retrieves of any dead game for the pup to conquer any repugnance it may have felt at the start.

By this time the youngster is very close to the stage where it could be sent to retrieve a freshly shot bird. The training programme now should be increasingly nearer to the real thing. By this time the pup will have been well grounded in its initial training. It will understand the meaning of directional hand signals and respond to the various whistles and commands without hesitation. It will drop to flush and shot, except when retrieving, and is reliably steady in most circumstances that it has so far encountered.

Firing shots and throwing dummies, or using an assistant to do so, or a dummy launcher, the trainer should now be able to walk out with the pup and set out three or more retrieves at various points of the compass. The pup may then be sent out to retrieve them in turn at considerable distances, upwind or down. The pup should also be able to retrieve across obstacles such as fences, hedges, or walls, on command, whether the dummy is thrown, or unseen. It should also be able to retrieve from, or across, water and from cover. So far, however, the bulk of its retrieving has been on the dummy, although it has been introduced to dead birds.

Once the pup has reached this stage and has begun to retrieve dead game the next important step is to introduce it to distasteful objects such as crows. When the pup can retrieve a dead crow without mouthing, or signs of distaste, it may be felt that it is coming close to being a trained retriever. There are, however, still some major points to be learned. In the meantime the majority of the lessons where a dummy was used may now be practiced with a crow, or similar bird, used in its place, although the same bird should not be used more than once as this can cause mouthing, or refusal to retrieve. Until the pup has considerable practice it is probably wise to keep away from woodpigeons as their loose feathers are very liable to cause mouthing. The first introductions to dead rabbits and hares should also be conducted with care.

The final stage of the retrieving training is teaching the youngster to retrieve a runner. In several countries in Europe it is permissible to send the youngster after a pinioned duck, or pheasant, with, or without, a minor cut to draw blood and so leave a blood trail. Apart from the obvious cruelty of such proceedings, they áre really quite unnecessary and not very efficient. It is perfectly feasible to reproduce an entirely realistic trail of wounded game and ensure that the pup is successful. Furthermore, since the trainer knows where the trail has been laid it is possible to assess the pup's performance accurately and gain a good idea of its abilities, which in the case of a pinioned bird is not by any means so easy.

It is important when laying a trail to ensure that the trainer's own scent in no way interferes with it. The fact is that for most of the retrieves so far, except those where the dummy has been thrown by an assistant, or where the dummy launcher has been used, the youngster has quite often probably followed the trainer's scent to the dummy, or at least to the throwing point. Care must now be taken that the pup only follows the scent that is laid for it and as far as possible there should be no other conflicting scents around which might mislead, or aid, the pup.

A scent trail can be laid effectively with a good strong beach casting rod, or else a stout spinning rod. With a freshly shot bird, still bleeding, attached to the end of the line, the trainer should cast it to the point where the trail is intended to start. Then playing out line on the spinning reel the trainer should circle round until some fifty yards (46 m) or more upwind of the dead bird. The bird may then be reeled in until it can be lifted up, when a second bird with wings and neck folded into a broad rubber band round its body should be dropped on the spot where the trail ends. The trail is then ready.

If an assistant is available a trail may easily be laid over any distance, with breaks, or twists, as required. All that is required is two lengths of fifty to a hundred yards (46–91 m) of fishing line. The bird is attached to each line and the trainer and his assistant each take an end. They can then drag the bird either upwind or downwind and occasionally raise it off the ground to simulate breaks in the scent. Finally one or other can release an end and the other then pulls the bird in to hand, whereupon a fresh, unbattered, bird, with wings and head folded into a rubber band is dropped on the spot. Because much longer trails can be organised in this way and breaks easily simulated to make the trail as difficult as is wished, this is probably the better method of the two, but very effective trails may also be laid by one person using only a fishing rod.

In the first instance, when a simple unbroken, trail has been laid downwind, the trainer should then fetch the pup and with the appropriate command and wave of the hand in the required direction set the pup on the retrieve. Almost certainly the trainer will learn a good deal from the pup's performance. This is very probably the first time that the trainer has been able to watch the pup actually working out a scent trail knowing where it should go in advance. The speed at which the pup will move is usually a revelation to the novice trainer and it is interesting to note such points as the effect of a side wind carrying the scent some yards from where the actual trail was laid, or how the pup copes naturally with a break in the trail by casting down wind to catch the scent. The trainer should almost always learn as much as the pup from such performances.

When the pup has retrieved the first bird laid in this manner, the trainer should have been able to make at least an initial assessment of its abilities and decided how to arrange the next trail accordingly. With a straightforward upwind trail there will have been little chance to do more than gauge the pup's general scenting abilities but this, in itself, should be a help. On the next occasion with one, or even two, breaks simulated, the pup should have a much more difficult task and this time the trainer will be able to decide more clearly which are its strengths and weaknesses. It may be that it is inclined to go too fast for its nose and is liable to overshoot the trail accordingly. In that case a few breaks, continued some yards downwind will teach it to work its ground carefully. This, as least,' is a failing caused by over confidence. When the pup shows itself easily at fault the important point is to build up its confidence by keeping the trails

Teaching pup to sit to command and whistle from an
early age by example. Dunpender Olga sitting to
command when ten weeks old, Dam Dunpender Meg
centre and Grandam Dunpender Lucy at left.

Teaching the pup to ignore poultry.

Use of a wall to teach the pup correct heel position.

Dropping at a distance to whistle and raised hand command using extending lead and dam to set example.

After dropping to whistle and command on extending lead. About to call in to heel by whistle and hand tapping knee.

Dropping to hand and whistle without lead.

Teaching the pup to remain dropped while handler crosses fence.

Teaching the pup to cross only on command and whistle.

Dropping the pup to shot and whistle with dam
setting example. (Using 28 bore for convenience and
early introduction to shot.)

Dam setting example to pup of retrieving dummy
and ignoring distractions of pigeon decoys.

Throwing dummy into long stubble while restraining
pup for early retrieve.

Pup sent off for decoy on command ignoring pigeon decoys.

Pup returning at speed with dummy to hand and ignoring pigeon decoys.

Dam returning with cock pheasant to hand after shot fired and watched by pup.

Dam points pheasant in hedge and pup backs while handler steadies her by stroking her gently.

Pup coming on early point is encouraged to remain
steady by handler.

Dam entering water to retrieve pigeon setting example to pup.

Dam returning from water retrieve with pigeon.

Grandam, dam and pup about to start work in a field
of rape with the pup on extending lead.

Handler advancing to flush bird in front of grandam
on point while pup remains firm backing on
extending lead and dam is also backing.

Grandam on point on one bird in background and
dam on point on another in foreground. Pup backing
grandam firmly on extending lead.

comparatively simple at first. The trainer may also give assistance as and when it is required, but should be careful not to interfere except as a last resort in case the pup becomes too reliant on his help.

As the pup advances so the trails may be made more difficult. If required they may be led to water and even over water. They may also be led to roads and over, or alongside them. They may be led to hedges, or fences, and through or over them. As far as possible the likely tricks of wounded game should be copied. Thus when coming to a stream, or road, the pup should be taught to work both sides to pick up the trail again. Where a difficult trail is laid the trainer should, of course, follow the pup's progress and where it is in real trouble may help it with whistle and signal. On the other hand it should be stressed again that it is highly undesirable that the pup should start to rely on the trainer and it is always best to leave it to puzzle matters out for itself rather than err on the side of helping it too much.

The aim of the training is to build up a gundog confident in its powers, yet willing to work in partnership with its trainer in the field. Whereas it is essential that the dog should obey any whistles and commands the trainer may give it, especially when it comes to directing it to the fall of game, once it is on a scent it should be in the best position to work out where the wounded bird, or beast, has gone. It is then desirable that the handler should rely on it to do the best it can. There is nothing worse than a handler who is constantly interfering with his dog in such conditions unless it is a dog which constantly looks to its handler to direct it because it is incapable of working out the scent for itself.

As far as retrieving goes, if the trainer has followed the stages outlined so far, the youngster should at least have had a good grounding. When it comes to working on the real thing it should have the necessary confidence and experience to be successful. Even so it is important to make the introduction a gradual one. To take a young dog, however well trained it may appear to be, and start it at a full day's driven shoot, or even a mixed rough shoot, is only asking for trouble. However good the youngster may appear at this stage it is still only half trained. There is a vast amount of experience still to be gained before it can be considered fully trained.

POSSIBLE WEEKLY TRAINING SCHEDULE: ADVANCED RETRIEVING:

First Week:

Introduce two dummies thrown, one after each other with commands 'Mark one' and 'Mark two'. Retrieves kept upwind for first week: Hand signals emphasised; alternate trainer fetching dummy and pup: Trainer carrying gun and accepting retrieve with free hand: Dummy thrown as pup out in front with shot fired. Pup marking.

Second Week:

Distractions introduced in shape of rolling dummy and then second dummy thrown as first retrieved: Shot also introduced as distraction; pup completing retrieves, but also still dropping to shot and rolling dummy in open: First retrieve from water: Going on to retrieving from over water with shot fired: Introduction to nettles and brambles for retrieves from cover; also from over fence, with command 'Fetch over': Variations in daily retrieving practice now very considerable.

Third Week:

Retrieving two dummies from water to hand signals: More retrieves over obstacles – hedges, ditches, walls: Now retrieving dummy from several hundred yards after command 'Mark' given and walking on: Starting on unseen retrieves, downwind and upwind: Advance to retrieving unseen over obstacles and across water: Command 'Over' and hand signals for direction now fully understood.

Fourth Week:

Introduction to first dead retrieves: Old partridges suitably bound with rubber band; mallard in water: Retrieving three dummies from different points of compass, seen and unseen:

Directed by hand signals, commands and whistle; varied retrieving practice with distractions and using crows: Preparing first trail for pup to follow: Successful upwind without breaks over hundred yard trail: Training now providing endless variety.

Fifth and Sixth Weeks:

Laying further trails with breaks; watching pup working out scent; assessing abilities under different scenting conditions: Varying retrieves, seen and unseen, over obstacles, across water: Adding trails with breaks on far side of both where pup in full view all the time: Fur as well as feather now used: Pup very steady despite distractions even when following trail: Very close to being ready for field as retriever.

6 Hunting and Pointing

The object of the hunting and pointing training described in this chapter is firstly to teach the youngster to 'quarter its ground with truth and judgement'. This somewhat hackneyed stock phrase to describe what is required is probably double-dutch to the average novice. In practice it means a lot more than is at first apparent. It means that the youngster must learn to understand and interpret correctly the myriad scents it will encounter during its work. It means that it must learn not to false point. This in turn means that it must learn not to point such things as larks, a common failing since their scent is obviously misleading at first. Nor must it point where game has been recently lying, although the scent may be extremely fresh. It must learn also to distinguish the scent of wounded game from that of unwounded game. It must learn to distinguish between game birds and groundgame. In short it must learn all that it possibly can about scent.

At the same time it must learn to quarter the ground correctly, as required by its handler, covering all likely places where game may lie within the bounds indicated to it. This means it must cover the ground in a series of long parallel runs into the wind obeying its handler's whistle when it has covered the required distance on each run. It must learn also to use the wind to its maximum advantage. This means that it must always quarter into the wind, from whichever direction it may be coming, whether from ahead, from the side, or behind. At the end of each run when turning on to the next parallel, it must turn into the wind, rather than downwind thus wasting ground and energy, as well as possibly losing game. It must also learn to recognise the sort of ground favoured by game, such as small tussocks of cover, and investigate them thoroughly. All this and more is implied in that innocent seeming stock phrase concerning quartering.

So far it is only hunting that has been mentioned. The young-ster must also learn to point and hold the game, once it has been found. It must be taught to come firmly and rigidly on point without drawing on, or moving forward, until the trainer gives the command, unless the game itself is moving forward. Then it should follow slowly, drawing forward on point. It must not, however, be allowed to become sticky on point, remaining rigid and refusing to move forward on command. Once the trainer gives the command the youngster must learn to move in and flush the game. It must be taught not to try to peg (or seize) the game, but allow it to flush freely. It must then honour the flush by dropping.

As will be seen from the above, scent is a major factor in both hunting and pointing. What is usually referred to simply as 'nose', is the pup's reaction to scent. The greater its 'nose', the greater its ability. To assess the pup's 'nose' it is essential that the trainer understands what causes scent and how the dog reacts to it. Basically, of course, whenever any animal puts a foot to the ground it is, willy-nilly, creating a scent trail which can be followed. However, as anyone who has every watched hounds following a scent will testify it is not necessarily only to be found at ground level. Some scents are clearly airborne and may be scented with the head held high. It is important to distinguish between these air scents, which may be followed with head up, and ground scents, distinguishable only with the head down, for they make a considerable difference to the way a dog hunts.

The hound following its quarry, when it comes to a break in the scent, will often put its nose down and puzzle out the ground scent, although at other times following an airborne scent. When quartering the ground in most conditions it is desirable that the pointer-retriever should work mainly on airborne scent, like any fast moving hunting dog, as opposed to a slow ground scenting dog. It should thus quarter its ground with head held high to receive air scents, rather than head held low following ground scents. When a pointer-retriever is working with head held low this may either mean that scent is poor, or else that the dog is more accustomed to working ground scent than air scent.

It is hard for modern human beings with their scenting instincts so very atrophied to understand the effect of scent on a dog. There must be so many fresh, intoxicating, new scents experienced by a pup each day that it would be very understandable if it became totally confused. Amazingly quickly, however, it learns the meaning of each of them, so that as it goes for a walk, it can, in effect, register the meaning of each scent it encounters, while barely pausing.

On each outing the pup is probably mentally registering something on the lines of: 'Ah, the ginger tomcat from next door passed this way last night. There is where it killed a mouse and here are some of the guts left behind. And here's where that black collie bitch down the road saw him and chased him up that tree. . . .' and so on. It is up to the trainer to become accustomed as soon as possible to the pup's reactions so that each check, or pause, each movement of the head, in turn tells the story of what its nose is unravelling. This is part of the two way communication between dog and trainer.

The microscopic particles which compose scent are, of course, subject to immense variations dependent on a great number of outside factors. It is only necessary to think of smoke from a bonfire which is, after all, scent in a visible form, and consider how it is affected by weather conditions and wind. If it is raining the smoke tends to be damped down. If the weather is very hot and sunny the smoke tends to be absorbed into the atmosphere. If there is no wind the smoke rises slowly. If there is much wind the smoke stays more or less level with the ground, but disperses quickly. Then again some smoke is denser than other smoke, as some scents are stronger than others due to the presence of more microscopic particles in the air.

To carry the analogy further, smoke will adhere to some surfaces more readily than others and the atmospheric conditions can have a considerable effect on this factor. So it is with scent. It may thus be appreciated that the microscopic particles composing scent, while not a tangible thing, or normally visible, are very much present in the air and on the ground, adhering faintly to most surfaces. They are emitted by all animals, including man, and are particularly emitted by game which is being hunted. In practice game is likely to emit quite different scents when it is undisturbed, when it is alarmed, when it is hunted, when it is wounded, or when it is dead. Scent, in these various forms, is the principal link between game and the gundog.

It is important therefore that the trainer should learn as much about scent as possible, the better to help the gundog when conditions are bad and to understand its reactions at all times. For instance the effect of temperature on scent is important. Thus both air and soil should contain a certain degree of moisture to retain the scent particles and for the best results each should be about the same temperature. Obviously enough if the temperature of the air is above that of the soil the particles will tend to rise, whereas if the soil temperature is higher the scent tends to remain at ground level.

It also applies that in general extreme weather conditions are bad for scent. If there is too much rain scent may be washed away, whereas if it is too dry the scent may rise quickly, or fail to lie at all. If it is very windy then scent may simply disappear. As a general rule when the ground is hard and the air is dry scent will not lie. Wherever the ground is changing condition, as on ploughland with a drying wind, amongst decaying leaves, or vegetation, during a thaw, or when a frost is drying off the ground, or more obviously amongst roots which have been frosted and smell strongly, or are dry and dusty, scent will not hold.

The trainer may usually expect scenting conditions to be reasonable when there is a light southerly, or west wind, providing mildly warm and moist conditions. On the whole dew, or a light mist, or fog, usually do not seem to produce bad scenting conditions, presumably because the scent particles stick to the moisture. In frosty weather scent will usually rise slightly, tending to produce a good effect, hence the condition known as 'a breast high scent'. The best way at any time to judge the scenting conditions, however, is to watch the dog's own reactions. Where it appears at all hesitant it may generally be assumed that scenting conditions are not good.

On the other hand there are certain occasions when it may not be the scent that is at fault, but the dog itself. For instance when a dog is off colour for any reason, as with a cold, it may partially, or even entirely, lose its 'nose'. Another not uncommon cause is when the dog has been fed some strong tasting food, as for instance someone's cheese sandwiches at a shooting lunch. If there is a lot of dust on the ground which is rising as the dog passes, such as ash from burned straw, or powder, or spore from dried roots, or pollen from heather, or flowers, coating the inside of the dog's nostrils, or if a bitch in season is working beside a dog, then little result can be expected.

When it comes to scent and scenting there are always a number of variable factors involved. The ground, the wind and the weather, in addition to the dog itself, have all to be considered at the start of each day. It is on the first three that the scent and behaviour of the game will to a large extent depend. Other factors that should be borne in mind are what the weather has been like in the previous twenty-four hours, for this too can have a considerable bearing on the reactions of the game.

Whether the pup is forward in pointing, or starts first by showing an inclination to retrieve, is a matter which is bound to vary from individual to individual even amongst those from the same litter. In general a forward pup may be seen to 'sight point' new and arresting spectacles from quite an early age, even while still with the dam. Such sight pointing is merely a momentary point when the pup has seen something that has caught its interest and momentarily freezes in position. Although not a proper point it is nevertheless a sign that the pup has a strong natural instinct in that direction.

It is really only where a pup comes naturally on point at frequent intervals that the trainer should take it in hand. There is always the possibility that if the instinct is not duly channelled when it becomes apparent in this way that the pup may get into the habit of drawing on (i.e. advancing slowly) and eventually of breaking its points and giving chase. Rather than take the risk of this, it is well worth encouraging the pup to point properly, especially since in many ways this tends to make other aspects of the training, such as the hunting and quartering, easier than might have been the case. It is always more satisfactory to know that if the dog is sent forward and encounters game it is likely to come on point rather than give chase.

Any pup which is naturally sight pointing from the age of two months or so is likely to start pointing between six and nine months at the latest. When the instinct will manifest itself is something that must vary from one individual to another. The first signs are likely to be a tendency to stiffen in sight points at poultry, or game. These sight points are likely to become more and more firm, until eventually the pup reaches the completely rigid state of the true point. It is probably then time to start pointing training, as will be outlined later in the chapter. It is more important initially, however, to ensure that the pup will drop at a distance to whistle and command. Prior to teaching the pup to quarter and hunt the long drop is essential. That should be the first aim.

Once the pup has been taught the first stage of its initial obedience training it should be encouraged to run free at a distance from the trainer. Undue dependence on the trainer and a tendency to return to heel without being told to do so should not be encouraged. As always a good deal must depend on the pup, but it is often more difficult to encourage a pup to move away from the trainer than might be thought. Once it is running free, however, the trainer should always make a point of changing direction abruptly at fairly frequent intervals and encouraging the pup to follow suit by whistle and hand signals. In this way the pup can often be taught to quarter its ground quite satifactorily without much more in the way of training, but this must never be overdone as the growing youngster may easily develop a weak heart.

By the time the secondary stage of obedience training has been completed limited quartering should be a regular feature of the training. The pup should be sent off with a wave of the hand into the wind, with the command 'Cast on'. When it reaches the distance that the trainer feels is correct a short whistle should be blown to attract the pup's attention. It should then be turned with a vigorous wave of the arm, pointing in the other direction. If at first it ignores the brief check whistle the long drop may be blown and the pup made to sit. The appropriate arm, pointing firmly in the required direction, and the command 'Cast on', should then set the pup moving correctly. This should be repeated whenever the pup shows signs of quartering too far on either side, until eventually it understands that when certain bounds are set at the start they should thereafter be adhered to unless the trainer wishes more ground to be covered. The novice trainer must remember, however, that, since it is going to point, the pup should be allowed well out of gunshot range, some fifty or more yards (45 m) on either side and some twenty to forty yards (18–37 m) in front. It should not be kept in too close. Hence the importance of not doing too much too young.

Where the pup has been too restricted and will not range out of gunshot it may be necessary to enlist the aid of two assistants in a suitably-sized field. With one on either side, about sixty yards (55 m) out from the trainer and about twenty to thirty yards (18–27 m) in front, they should walk forward into the wind. The pup should then be waved towards the first assistant, with the command 'Cast on'. The assistant should then call the pup. As it approaches that assistant the trainer should then call it once again and this time direct it with a decisive arm signal towards the other assistant, whose turn it now is to call the pup. Thus the trainer and assistants should walk up the field encouraging the pup to quarter its ground and get well out. It should be encouraged by the assistants to turn towards the wind, not back, and the trainer should urge it forwards and to each side. Usually the pup should not take along to respond to this training and increase its range.

So far reference has only been made to quartering the ground into the wind and as far as possible initially this is how the youngster should be worked, even when it is pointing quite firmly. When, however, it is felt it has gained sufficient experience it may be decided to quarter it with a side wind, blowing across the ground to be quartered. This means that the youngster then has to quarter the ground forwards and backwards, moving directly out from the trainer some eighty yards (73 m) or more, then turning into the wind and coming back again. In this way it should quarter an area of some fifty yards (45 m) wide in front of the trainer as they advance together. With the wind directly behind the trainer, the pup must be encouraged to go some eighty to a hundred yards (73–91 m) forward and then quarter the ground back to the trainer, thus finding any game between them, but still working into the wind. Whatever direction the wind may be coming from, the pointer-retriever is said to be 'using the wind correctly' when it is working directly into it and taking the maximum advantage of it as an aid to scenting game.

Until the youngster shows signs of pointing firmly, as indicated earlier, the trainer may prefer not to start this aspect of training. On the other hand there are those who advocate encouraging the youngster to point before starting on the retrieving training. Quite a lot, as always, must depend on the individual pup and the individual trainer. Sometimes the circumstances are such that it would seem more sensible to concentrate on pointing first. This could be the case, for instance, where the trainer and pup went to stay on ground not normally available to them where plenty of game was available for practice. In the event it will probably be the case that to some extent the training programme decides itself and the youngster may well be receiving initial obedience training in its final stages at the same time as both retrieving and pointing training.

In any event, once the youngster has reached the stage of being successfully trained to quarter the ground, it is highly desirable to encourage the pointing aspect of the training soon afterwards. This is, indeed, then clearly essential since it is not easy to guarantee that the pup will always be quartering areas completely devoid of ground game. However well the initial obedience training may have gone it is certainly not a good thing to have the youngster ruining it by falling for the temptation of starting to chase rabbits, or hares, before it has learned to point. Quite apart from any other considerations this will only make it harder to encourage the pointing instinct. Once the youngster learns of the thrills of giving chase to game, even where it has already learned to point, the problems facing the trainer are likely to be considerable, to put it mildly.

For example, the youngster I took back to train for the doctor soon proved a superlative dog. Not only would it quarter its ground well, covering a wide range at speed, hunting it in text-book style, it also had an excellent nose and froze into a classic point on encountering the scent of either fur, or feather. It was a natural worker, both as a retriever and pointer, and I did my best to persuade the doctor to let me have it back for double the price he had paid for it. Unfortunately by this time he had seen the dog working and he refused obstinately to sell it back to me, as, of course, was his right, but I did at least insist on him coming to learn how to handle it. His total inability to praise the youngster raised my worst fears, but eventually after three months I had to part with it, by which time it was up to field trial winning standard. Even with the doctor handling it the young-ster was behaving perfectly.

I might have known what would happen. Although the doctor had promised faithfully to exercise it regularly and not allow it to roam free within six months I heard reports of it being seen wandering loose on the outksirts of the city and eventually I had a telephone call asking me to take it back. By then, if it saw a lark in flight at a hundred yards (91 m) or more, and it had keen sight, it simply took off in pursuit. In order to prevent it being put down, since I felt its plight was my fault and because I had faith in the dog itself, I took it back. The process of curing it of the vices it had been allowed to learn was a lengthy and difficult one and at times seemed to verge on the impossible. It cannot be over-stressed that once a youngster has learned to give chase and to self-hunt it is extremely hard to cure. Prevention is always the simplest and sometimes the only cure in such cases.

As will have been gathered the introduction to game might seem to present problems, when it comes to training the dog to point. In practice there is really nothing difficult about it. The important thing is to gain access to a pigeon loft. With a plentiful supply of pigeons the problem of training the youngster to hunt its ground and point becomes comparatively simple. Where there are no pigeons available and it is decided to train the youngster on wild game only a good deal depends on how much game is available and whether the trainer can be sure of finding it as and when required. On a well stocked shoot the problem is not a difficult one, but even so the use of pigeons does have the advantage of knowing in advance exactly where the dog should pick up a scent and come on point. In the initial lessons, when training the dog to point, this is a very distinct advantage.

When using pigeons to train the youngster to point three methods may be used. The pigeons may be inserted in wire netting cages, hidden in clumps of grass. They may be inserted in holes, scooped in the ground, and covered with a square of wire netting, or an ordinary roof slate. Alternatively, and possibly best of all, they may be dizzied, by simply tucking the head under the wing, then rocking the bird on its back gently and placing it carefully on the ground. Pigeons, or indeed most birds, dizzied in this way will lie quiescent for up to twenty minutes, which is usually more than enough time to go back, fetch the youngster, quarter the ground with it and bring it onto point. If the bird is taken from a pigeon loft it will, of course, duly return when stirred into flight and may then be used again another time. It should perhaps be mentioned that it is illegal, and rightly so, to use any form of tether to keep the bird in position. Nor is it necessary, or desirable, to do so since any of the methods mentioned are much more effective.

Whichever method of setting out pigeons is used, the birds should have a stick marker stuck in the ground close to them to ensure that the trainer can tell within a few inches where they have been placed. In this way it is possible to quarter the ground into the wind and know when the youngster should be scenting the bird. The trainer can thus anticipate the pup's reactions and prepare for them. If there is initially any doubt about whether it will stop on scenting the game, the trainer should work the pup with a check lead in position ready for use if necessary.

When the trainer decides that the bird has been scented the youngster should be checked gently. Thereafter the pup may be allowed to approach slowly towards the bird and the trainer should close gently up on it at the same time, until eventually it is at a standstill. By that time the trainer should be right up on the pup while its attention is wholly focused on the bird. It should be sufficient at first to hold the youngster steady in position for a minute or two. Then the trainer should stroke the pup slowly and gently from the head right down to the tip of the tail. The whole approach should be slow and it is important not to rush up on the youngster as soon as it is seen to take the scent, for this can have the opposite effect to that desired.

Even if the pup does not immediately freeze solidly into the rigid state of a true point, the probability is that it will stand firm without movement. Continued gentle stroking will have the effect of steadying it gradually even more. The pup may then finally be led away and worked on until another bird is reached, when the performance may be repeated. By degrees, using this method, it is likely that a firm point will be achieved even in the case of breeds of dog which are not by nature pointers. The degree of firmness on point is, of course, something that varies with each dog, even of pointing, or setting, breeds. It should be appreciated, however, that the dog's semi-hypnotic trance on point is shared by the game, each aware of the other's presence and frozen rigid. The slightest movement at this stage breaks the spell.

If a more mature dog is brought in at this stage to come on point ahead of the youngster the effect can be considerable. The pup will very probably imitate the dog on point by stiffening rigidly at once. If at first it pays little or no attention, it is up to the trainer to steady it down on the check cord, as indicated, whenever it is plain that it too should have scented the game. The effect of example in such cases can be dramatic. I have even seen two miniature dachshunds which were in the habit of accompanying a pointer-retriever, backing it firmly, rigid as statues. They were self-taught, but where the youngster is brought up slowly behind another dog on point it should soon take to backing it.* There is, however, a danger that if this is overdone the pup may start blinking,* or losing interest.

Whether another dog is used to set an example, or whether the youngster is simply taken up on pigeons laid out for it until it points of its own accord, the process should not take very long if properly executed. The youngster, however, must not be allowed to press forward by degrees, drawing on, until its nose is right over the bird. If this is allowed the danger is that the pup will learn to

*see glossary p. 173

put its head down and peg the game. This must be prevented at all costs.

In practice once the pup has attained the truly rigid state of a firm point, the body is literally frozen into place. There is often considerable difficulty then in urging the pup onwards. Some dogs, of course, may never achieve this state, although any well bred pointer-retriever should have little difficulty in doing so. Once this has happened the dog will remain on point indefinitely and initially should be left in this rigid state for several minutes at least, with the trainer gently stroking and soothing it. If the youngster shows any tendency to lie down at this stage it should be gently restrained and, if possible, held up until pointing rigidly.

While the youngster is still learning to point firmly, as outlined above, it is, on the whole, desirable not to flush the birds in front of it. It is probably preferable to lead it away leaving the bird on the ground and taking it on to another, thus avoiding any extra distraction, for if the pigeon is flushed the youngster should drop, honouring the flush. At this stage, therefore, in some ways it is an advantage to use a caged bird.

Later, when the youngster is pointing reliably, several pigeons may be placed in a field, each marked with a twig, or wand of hazel. The pup should then be quartered across the field until it comes firmly on point. If it is some distance from the bird it may be urged gently closer. With a really rigid pointer at this stage especially it may be quite hard to make it obey the command 'On' and the gentle push of the hand on the back. It should, however, be urged onwards until close enough to the bird for it to be flushed by the trainer. The pup should then honour the flush by dropping at once.

If the pigeons are dizzied birds it only requires a prod with the trainer's toe to break the spell and urge them into flight. If caged or under a slate, a length of fishing line should have been attached to it and laid downwind so that the trainer, by pulling on the line can release the bird as the dog is urged forward, drawing on, on point. In each case a shot should be fired in the air after the bird has taken flight to simulate the flush of game and shot. The pup, of course, should drop to both. In the case of either a bird in a cage, or under a slate, the scent is sometimes inclined to be obscured, but compared with a dizzied bird it is usually easier to arrange the flush by either of these methods.

The stage has now been reached where the youngster should be fit to take out over any ground and quarter freely, hunting in search of game. On encountering such game it should automatically come on point, freezing rigidly in classic stance. It is possible, when training the youngster to point, to teach it to raise a foreleg for feather and a hind for fur. This is, in any event, often a natural reaction, but it is a refinement which really can be omitted. As long as the youngster scents its game and points rigidly as soon as it does so, without flushing it before the trainer is within range, that is as much as anyone should expect.

As it quarters its ground the pup should automatically turn into the wind on the trainer's whistle and signal. Any attempt to turn back and downwind should be firmly checked as not only less stylish, but also less efficient. When game is flushed accidentally it should also automatically drop at once, whether to fur, or feather. Each day out should see a steady improvement in the youngster's style as its experience grows and it works increasingly in tune with its trainer.

The trainer too should be learning the ways of his pup as it progresses. Soon it will be clear to the trainer when it has scented ground game as opposed to a gamebird. There will be a distinct and appreciable difference in the pup's reaction. The same will be true when it hesitates at a point where game has been flushed, or lain overnight. By watching it constantly the trainer will gradually come to understand what each pause, or hesitation, each half point, or check, means. The youngster will thus be communicating continuously with its trainer throughout the day, just as much as the trainer is communicating with the pup by means of whistles and signals.

By this time exercising the youngster should be no problem. With each day out its experience will be expanding along with its understanding of what the trainer wants of it. With increasing practice it will soon understand that it is intended to draw on, when on point, only as required by the trainer. However firmly it may be on point it should draw slowly forward at the trainer's command 'On' and a gentle wave of the hand forward. If there is any tendency towards stickiness on point (i.e. refusal to move forward when urged) this should soon be overcome with regular practice. It is in any event a preferable fault to over eagerness to move in to the game, which can lead to unsteadiness and should be carefully restrained. Initially at least, as indicated, the trainer should flush the game for the youngster, to avoid this latter fault. As the pup becomes more reliable, however, it should be possible to advance a stage further.

Although wild game will generally flush of its own volition with the close approach of the trainer and dog there are occasions when, for instance, a rabbit will clap down instinctively (i.e. lie down hoping to be overlooked). On such occasions, initially at least, it is best that the trainer should flush it with his foot, ahead of the dog. On the other hand, by using dizzied pigeons, it is possible to simulate this situation and encourage the youngster to put its nose under the game and flush it when urged to do so. Any attempt to sieze the dizzied pigeon in its jaws should be firmly checked with the command 'No'. Thus, by degrees, the pup will come to appreciate what is required of it. In these circumstances it will not attempt to sieze the game, but will instead put its nose under it and flush it.

By this time, if it has completed its retrieving training as well, the youngster should be very close to the stage where it may be shot over. It will be quartering its ground taking the range chosen by its trainer, as a variable-range pointer-retriever should. Inevitably in cover its pace will be slower than in the open, but it will generally work at the speed its nose permits. This may well vary with different scenting conditions. The important point is that the youngster should not miss game. If it has been trained on the lines indicated the trainer should have a very fair assessment of its character and ability and above all of its nose.

Just how far the retrieving and the hunting and pointing training have been synchronised will inevitably vary from pup to pup and trainer to trainer. Some will take an inordinate time over aspects of the training which another will learn immediately. No two trainers, or their charges, are alike. All that can be said is that, if the lessons are absorbed steadily and the initial obedience training has been thoroughly inculcated, by the time the youngster has reached this stage in training it should have a very good grounding.

This is not to say that all these preparations cannot very easily be wasted and the pup ruined by pressing on too hard too soon, or by a certain amount of carelessness on the trainer's part. The old trainer's saying 'Months to make and minutes to spoil' still holds good. It is important never to push any youngster, however willing, too hard. No pup, however mature it might seem should be expected to work seriously before it is a year to eighteen months old. At under two years the youngster still has a lot to learn.

POSSIBLE WEEKLY TRAINING SCHEDULE:
HUNTING AND POINTING:

First Week:

Training pup in quartering ground by changing direction regularly and waving pup on in required direction. By trainer zig-zagging pup quartering not too badly: Using obedience training give command 'Cast on' and use long drop to make pup halt when required then sending in opposite direction with command and wave of arm: By steady use of whistle and command pup quartering reasonably well; still turning downwind occasionally at end of run: Sight pointing and nearly rigid at times.

Second Week:

Using two assistants give youngster intensive session in quartering: Turning up wind at end of runs by finish: Then using caged birds bring pup on point on check lead; soothe and stroke all over from head to tail: Pup beginning to freeze into rigid point: Use older dog for one session and pup freezes rigidly backing: Thereafter comes on rigid point on its own: Dizzied birds now being used in field and several points achieved: No attempt as yet to flush birds.

Third Week:

Pup brought up on point on check lead and urged on to flush bird; dizzied pigeon flushed by point of trainer's shoe, pup dropped to flush, honouring flush of bird: Used pigeon under slate as well and pup soon accustomed to dropping to flush: When fully satisfied no danger of pup drawing on too hard and spoiling rigid point will urge on to flush: Seems extremely rigid on point at present: Nose outstanding as already seen by retrieving ability.

Fourth Week:

Taken out on shoot and pointed brace of partridges; honoured flush by dropping; completely rigid on point though drew on until only two or three yards (1.8–2.7 m) from birds: Urged on to flush and as soon as pup moved birds flushed: Several points on dizzied birds successful: Quartering now reliable into wind: may consider trying pup with cheek wind to see reactions.

Fifth and Sixth Weeks:

Use of gun in addition to flush of game ensuring drop; pup urged forward to flush dizzied birds and with warning 'No' making no attempt to peg them; birds flushed and flush honoured by dropping: Tried with cheek wind and worked instinctively almost correctly; runs a little ragged, but came on point to dizzied pigeons: No game missed: Watching pup quartering ground it is interesting to note reactions to where game has been; pointing larks, but after warning 'No' has made no further mistakes: Classic point with foreleg raised on pheasant: Dropping nose on scent when crossing line of hare, but no other notice taken: Near point where partridges had been, but after check continued: Sound working ability.

7 Advanced Training

When the young pointer-retriever has reached the stage of being shot over in earnest at last, the trainer should appreciate that this is not the coping stone of its training, but rather the foundation stone. As a variable-range, variable-pace, pointer-retriever it has its whole life in front of it. It is still very young and is almost certainly not grown to its full strength. There is still a great danger of overdoing either the work, or the training, and souring even the most willing of pups. The trainer's aim should now be to take every opportunity to increase the youngster's experience and introduce it to new forms of shooting whenever available, so that it becomes a genuine all-round hunting dog.

It is desirable to start it, if possible, in July and August on the moor, ranging wide and learning the scent of grouse and blackgame, as well as snipe in the boggy ground. The fluttering of young grouse just over the heather tops is a tempting spectacle for the inexperienced youngster, as are partridge and pheasant cheepers on the low ground. Young grouse are also soft and feathery mouthfuls, which require a careful introduction. It is best to start the youngster on a tough old grouse of several seasons, rather than risk a possible fiasco on a tender and easily crushed young bird. The first introduction to snipe should also be treated with care. The youngster may not at first appreciate the taste of this small mouthful and may spit it out, or worse still crunch it.

Partridges on the fringes of the moor, on the stubbles, or in roots, may be tackled in September. Each presents a different ranging problem and as far as possible the youngster should be given as much experience on them as on grouse. Of course, this is not always possible and generally the youngster will gain much more experience on one than on the other. It is, however, true that a pointer-retriever started only on grouse is seldom as good on partridge, and vice versa. Although the youngster may later become a good worker on each it is always liable to show a slightly greater keeness on one or the other associated with this early training and experience.

If there is any possibility of shooting ptarmigan on the high tops in September, or capercailzie on the forest edges in October, these should certainly not be missed. Any chances of picking up at driven blackgame or capercailzie shoots should be taken if offered, even where it means lengthy and expensive drives from one end of the country to another. Low ground shooting on pheasants, ranging fields of roots and stubbles, in October and November, should follow, with more organised driven days as well.

Any opportunity to shoot wildfowl, retrieving from the tidal saltings, or inland reservoirs, or lochs, should also be taken if the chance arises. The more opportunities the youngster has for retrieving wildfowl in darkening, or dawn, the better. All such experiences will broaden its background knowledge and, as long as it is kept under control and not allowed to follow any bad examples it may be set, should do it nothing but good.

Regular outings, where it is meeting other dogs and learning to adapt to strange surroundings, travelling in trailers behind tractors, in vans with other animals and heaps of shot game all help to teach the youngster its task. It must become accustomed to being wet and muddy, hungry and tired, but still not complain. In strange countryside it must learn to keep one eye on its master and handler while quartering its ground and finding game. It must learn to adapt itself to a line of guns and not to interfere with other dogs, or their retrieves. When other dogs chase hares, or rabbits, it must learn to stay steady. It must disregard temptation and remember its training. If that training has been conscientiously carried out it is surprising how much temptation it will in fact be able to withstand.

If the trainer at this stage becomes too interested in the shooting and concentrates on this rather than the dog, as is very easily done, all the time that has been spent on training might just as well have been wasted. The chances are that without the trainer's eye watching it at this critical period in its development the young dog will begin to pick up bad habits. It will start ignoring the stop whistle. It will start running in to fall of game. It will not always drop to shot, or flush. In short by degrees its months of training will subtly be undermined.

It cannot be emphasised too strongly that during the first season the trainer should carry a gun only occasionally and then rather with a view to giving the youngster useful experience than to filling the bag. There will be many seasons more to come when these precautions will pay off handsomely. It is only by keeping a close eye on the young dog when it is introduced to its first full scale shooting season that the trainer can hope to keep it steady.

The first time that a young dog experiences a driven day, with birds falling all around and the constant sound of shots, is in itself an experience it is virtually impossible to simulate in training. Without the trainer's guidance and restraint the young gundog would be totally bewildered and could well run wild, causing considerable annoyance to others and possibly spoiling part of the day's sport. Most sportsmen will have seen some such exhibition when a dog which its owner thought fully trained has behaved deplorably in full view of an entire shooting party and it is not an experience anyone would care to undergo voluntarily. Nor does it do the dog any good. Altogether it is to be avoided.

Certain aspects of training, for which the pup has had a brief preparation, but which have not been thoroughly followed through can now be thoroughly tested. In particular the young pointer-retriever should be worked in cover, in what amounts to a spaniel role. Initially it will tend, almost certainly, to point in cover and this is where experience only can teach it what is required of it. The important point here is to find a good training area, where the ground provides cover, but in limited patches, so that the dog is not totally lost to the trainer's view. Small, not too thick patches of gorse, or whin, with a few rabbits in them are ideal for training. The trainer, of course, should not initially carry a gun, but should concentrate on helping the dog. One or more friends who are safe shots should be enough to deal with the rabbits that are bolted from the cover.

With a gun on either side of a suitable small patch of cover the trainer should wave the dog into it, giving the command 'Cast in'. He should then attempt to keep as close a watch on the dog's actions as possible. If the youngster comes on point the trainer should enter the cover and urge it to push the rabbit out. As soon as the rabbit breaks cover, however, the trainer must make the dog drop at once. The gun it is to be hoped will then bowl the rabbit over and after a pause the dog may be sent to retrieve it. By urging the pup on inside the cover and ensuring that whenever it goes into the open it is made to drop it is likely that in the end it will understand what is required of it. This training, however, is so counter to everything it has been taught previously that it is best left until the end of the first season, or even well into the next, when it is fully experienced and steady. If the trainer has access to a rabbit pen such as is used by professional trainers this is useful initially but is no substitute for the real thing.

Throughout the first season the young pointer-retriever should constantly be expanding its experience. The first encounter with a woodcock, a bird which has a peculiarly displeasing taste to most gundogs, is one of those small milestones in any youngster's life. There will not usually be any trouble about the point, for the woodcock is certainly a gamey enough bird. Once it is shot, however, the youngster may show a distinct distaste for the retrieve. This is, however, a good test of the preliminary training and if the youngster has retrieved crows and starlings, also unpleasant tasting birds, there should be no real problem with a woodcock.

The pointer-retriever will also automatically come on point at both fox and roe. If shooting in a non-hunting country where foxes are shot it may be that one is shot in front of the youngster. A certain amount of care should be taken that it is dead before sending the youngster in to retrieve it. Most pointer-retrievers will not only face up to a fox, but will, if necessary, kill it as they are mostly taught to do in their native lands, just as they are also taught to track and pull down roe. Although this may not affect their mouths when retrieving game birds, neither of these are attributes generally required in this country.

In Germany, however, the pointer-retriever is also taught the

'Umschlagen', which literally means the break-round. When an old bird is running persistently in front, the experienced dog, drawing on fast behind it, may literally break away, at a wave of the hand from its trainer, and with head held high and body low, will run forward and head off the running bird, holding it between itself and the handler. This is a remarkable feat, which can be taught, where it is not instinctive, but requires suitable circumstances for doing so. With a second or third season dog, as it is drawing on after a bird which is persistently running ahead, the trainer may attract its attention and wave it to one side and forward with an emphatic gesture. An intelligent natural worker may then realise what is required and accomplish the feat. It is not something that should be expected from a young dog.

Some thirty years ago my first G.S.P. dog, Max, taught me how this remarkable 'Umschlagen' worked one day when we were following a fast moving old cock pheasant in thick stubble. The bird was running fast ahead of us and suddenly Max, who was drawing on fast, glanced round at me, although I had never before known him show any signs of distraction when on point. It was obvious, however that he was merely making sure that I was watching, for the next moment, on his own initiative, he slipped away sideways, with his head held high and his body sunk low to the ground with a most peculiar looking action. Suddenly speeding up he moved forward fast and within a few seconds was standing firmly on point some forty yards (37 m) from me looking now straight back towards me. The cock pheasant thus headed, had no choice but to fly when I advanced towards it and was duly downed, to be retrieved in due course by a suitably pleased Max with a justifiable air of 'Wasn't that something?'

Surprisingly enough I once had a similar experience with the dog already mentioned which I took back from the doctor. It had already distinguished itself on several occasions by taking off and disappearing into the distance, so on this occasion it was firmly anchored to my person on a slip lead slung over one shoulder. Coming to a small quarry a very large dog fox suddenly erupted from the other side. I fired both barrels and bowled it over, for this is a non-hunting country. Unfortunately it picked itself up and continued on slowly out of range bleeding profusely. There was nothing for it but to let the dog go. I duly did so and to my surpise he immediately gave chase and almost at once headed the fox, crowding it round until he brought it snarling and bloody within some four feet (1.2 m) of me, whereupon I despatched it cleanly with another shot.

Such experiences are, of course, uncommon and likely to be remembered for a long time. They are the product of the dog's instincts and the trainer should learn from them and if possible apply them where it may be useful to do so. For the most part, however, the trainer should be introducing the youngster to different aspects of shooting, where its natural instincts may need restraining or channelling into slightly different lines.

This is very much the case, for example, with any form of shooting over decoys whether for pigeons, or for the various forms of wildfowl. While a properly trained dog can be extremely useful on such occasions, watching from the hide and marking the fall of the birds, it can also be a considerable nuisance if it is not properly trained. An ill-behaved animal which rampages out of the hide at the first shot, refusing to return when called, frightening off further incoming birds and upsetting the carefully placed decoys, possibly even retrieving them, is nothing more than a liability. Yet it does not require much training to change the picture entirely.

When pigeon shooting over decoys it is necessary first to make sure that the young dog understands that it is not to retrieve the birds, or decoys, set out. Whether ordinary dead pigeons are used, as is commonly the case, with their necks propped on sticks, or wire, rather than artificial fibre, or rubber, decoys, the young dog should be shown them in position before any attempt is made to start shooting. The youngster should be allowed to inspect them all with a firm prohibitive 'No' for each. If it is felt desirable, for the trainer's peace of mind, rather than for the dog's sake, a drop of some evil smelling compound such as one of the proprietary anti-fox liquids, or anti-mate, on each will clearly distinguish the decoys from any freshly shot birds which may fall amongst them. In practice any birds which have

already been handled by the trainer will be clearly distinguishable to the dog's nose. It is merely a question of impressing
on the animal that these are not to be retrieved.

The best method of ensuring that the youngster understands
what is required when shooting over decoys is for the trainer to
make a point of retrieving the first birds that fall, rather than
sending the dog to do so. This should be repeated for any birds
falling close to, or amongst, the decoys and initially the dog
should only be sent for any birds that fall well wide of them.
Should the youngster show any sign of approaching the decoys a
firm 'No' must be given. It should not take more than a day or so
for the dog to understand that the decoys must not be touched.
Exactly the same principle applies to shooting wildfowl over
decoys, although in this case it is advisable to keep the youngster
firmly in to heel as darkness falls at evening flight during the first
few outings simply to avoid any possible errors being committed
while the trainer is unable to see clearly what is happening.

Another form of shooting which requires unnatural restraint
on the part of the young dog is ferreting. Here the really important point is that the youngster should get to know and recognise
the ferret as an animal which must not be touched. If the trainer
keeps ferrets this is simple enough. The gundog may be introduced to them from an early age and will become accustomed to
knowing that they are, in effect, part of the household. The
probability is that as a pup it will point the hutch in which the
ferrets live, but by use of the firm prohibition 'No' whenever
they are brought out the message should go home that they are
not to be touched. Where the youngster has never before seen
ferrets they should be carefully introduced to each other at the
first opportunity, before starting the day, with the prohibition
'No' to the dog. Thereafter it is advisable to keep it on the lead
during the first ferreting expedition, for the last thing required is
a dead, or injured, ferret.

Ferreting, however, is a sport where the few dogs used should
be steady and experienced. On the first outing or two the youngster should therefore, in any event, be kept on the lead as much
for its own safety as that of the ferret. Where one or two guns are
working a hedgerow, for instance, rabbits are liable to be bolting

on both sides with little warning and a young dog can very quickly become over excited and either start to chase, or disobey orders. In such a case a snap shot might easily have disastrous effects, killing, or injuring, a dog which had run in to fetch an injured rabbit and bringing to a sad end all the effort that has gone into its training.

Admittedly all guns at ferreting expeditions should be calm and experienced shots, but it is equally desirable that the dogs should also be calm and under control. For the first few outings the young dog should only be allowed to retrieve when it is entirely safe to do so. The experience of seeing rabbits bolting unexpectedly out of holes and breaking into the open to be bowled over by snap shots will in any event soon improve both his experience and his steadiness.

It is certainly only when the young dog is reliably steady that it should be introduced to hare shoots. These are liable to be large and, by virtue of their size, somewhat unmanageable affairs. A number of wild dogs, from collie crosses, to lurchers, may be present and one or two will almost certainly be setting a bad example by giving chase at some point during the day, whereupon another is likely to join in until eventually a pack is in full cry across the fields. Such sights are certainly not uncommon on these occasions and the shooting is not always of the best. It is highly desirable, therefore, if you value your dog and the time you have spent training together that you should keep it well under control on such outings.

If it has not already become accustomed to doing so, the young dog should now be introduced to spending the night in the car. Inevitably there will be times when it is necessary to drive long distances to shoot, possibly spending one or two nights in the course of the proceedings. Although there may be kennels available, or the dog may be allowed to sleep inside the house, possibly in a basket in its owner's room, this may not always be the case, even if it is so wished. There are many hotels, for instance, which refuse to allow dogs inside the premises and it is perfectly understandable that this should be the case. In such instances there may be no alternative to the dog spending the night in the car. If, however, it has a basket and suitable bedding, it should be as comfortable there as in its kennel at home. The only point is that as far as possible the car should be parked under cover, not entirely at the mercy of the elements, either baking hot sun, or freezing blizzards, and also somewhere relatively undisturbed. A dog which is accustomed to this arrangement is undoubtedly an asset, whereas in certain circumstances, if it cannot be trusted in the car, it becomes a distinct liability.

Whenever travelling, of course, the thoughtful dog owner will always carry sufficient food for the dog. Food and drinking bowls will also be carried as a matter of course and drinking water should also be kept in a container, in case none is readily available. In addition, naturally, the dog should be attended to after the day's shoot, dried off, if necessary, and fed, before the owner settles down to post-shoot mortems and drinks. Only too often one sees the spectacle of dogs in the backs of cars outside pubs, steaming up the windows as they dry off unheeded, wet and cold after a day's shooting, while their owners guzzle drinks and food inside. This is distinctly bad practice, if only because, like a car, or a human being, a dog will perform better if regularly cared for after work.

It is important as soon as possible after each day's outing, especially where the dog has been out of sight in cover, leaping barbed wire fences, or otherwise at risk, to check it over for possible injuries. Large thorns can be removed before they break off and start to cause infections. Small cuts, or grazes, can be dealt with at once with a dab of disinfectant. Deeper cuts, or stake wounds, may require more attention. In the case of ragged tears, or deep stakes, it may be necessary to go to the vet and such wounds should not be left until the following morning when the vet's surgery opens. They are best stitched at once with a sprinkle of sulphanilamide powder, or similar disinfectant, healing, antibiotic. Any injury to the dog discovered on the following day is a black mark against the owner.

In the case of sprains, or greenstick fractures, they are not always apparent during the day. When the dog eases off after work, however, they should be immediately obvious. Lameness will show very plainly, although it is not always easy to determine exactly where the seat of the pain lies. Especially in shoulder ailments, where a muscle has been badly pulled, for instance, the dog may refuse to put the foot on the ground and show pain whenever the leg is handled, thus making diagnosis difficult. It may be necessary to manipulate the leg firmly, manipulating each joint in turn, until the seat of the lameness is plain. In such cases it may be felt sufficient to rub the affected area with a good muscle embrocation such as Radiol. This may have to be repeated, but the effects the next day are often remarkable, whereas if not attended to at once such sprains may cause lameness for some time and may need considerable rest. Wherever there is any doubt, however, it is advisable to consult the vet.

When the young dog starts work seriously it is always going to encounter other dogs. It is, as has been indicated, an important part of its training that it should have met as many other dogs as possible in as varying situations as could be arranged. It should have been taught from the earliest age not to be quarrelsome and any tendency in this direction should have been promptly and firmly checked at the slightest sign of growling, or snarling. It should also have learned to travel with other dogs even allowing them into what it will have come to regard as its own car, a private domain akin to the kennel, or basket. It should also be prepared to watch them retrieving close at hand without evincing any jealousy or desire to interfere.

These are the ordinary aspects of training, which should be expected in every reasonably well trained youngster. It may well be, however, that the trainer has never had an opportunity to work his youngster in conjunction with another, in the full pointer-retriever role. In other words the youngster may have been trained to accept another dog working alongside it as a retriever, but has so far had little or no opportunity of working with another pointer. Of course it may even be that the position is exactly reversed and the youngster has worked with another pointer, but not with another retriever, although this is obviously a much less common state of affairs.

Where experience of working with another pointer-retriever is lacking, the trainer should include this in the youngster's education at the earliest opportunity. The chances are that the pup will take to it quite naturally, but where it has not been accustomed to many other dogs it may show signs of jealousy. This is precisely why such training is desirable. Unless the dog can be relied on to work with other dogs in the field in each and every aspect of the work for which it is intended, especially in its full pointer-retriever role, it cannot be regarded as fully trained.

Where the youngster is working with another pointer-retriever in the field for the first time it is usually desirable to start with an older dog if possible, since there is then likely to be less chance of jealousy intruding. With two youngsters of much the same age there can often be an element of jealousy leading to disobedience, or refusal to honour the other's points by backing, even a disposition to ignore the other dog on point and to steal the points from it. This can be very tiresome as in bad cases it may lead to deliberate disobedience.

The basic principle, however, should be for the two trainers to start alongside each other with their dogs and cast each of them off in opposite directions into the wind. The object then should be to try to get them to work their own ground individually, crossing each other, without paying any attention to the other. Any tendency on the part of either to follow the other dog, or leave part of its own ground uncovered, should be promptly checked. The dog should then be sent on to cover its own ground regardless of the other.

If either dog comes on point the other should be dropped immediately if it shows no sign of honouring the point by backing. It may then be slipped onto the lead and led up until it scents the game, whereupon it should also point. This procedure may have to be repeated several times with a dog of particularly jealous disposition, but finally it should be prepared to acknowledge the other's points by backing. If it persists in refusing to do so, it should merely be dropped each time the other points. With another pointer-retriever it may perform perfectly. Certainly as it matures and with experience such behaviour is likely to be forgotten. It is very typical of immaturity.

Although during its advanced training the trainer may decide occasionally to use dizzied birds, or even lay trails for the youngster to follow, to emphasise some aspect of training which appears to be weak, the time has really come where the dog is usually better trained on the real thing where possible. This is never to say that training should not be repeated from time to time, even with a fully grown dog where it appears to be in need of it. There is always some advantage to be gained from repeating even the most elementary of lessons at times, especially where any sign of disobedience has been noted.

The use of such things as dummy launchers and electronic collars, should not, however, be strictly necessary. Although the dummy launcher can have its uses, especially in working tests and training classes, primarily for convenience sake to avoid the use of an assistant, it should not really be necessary at this stage. Nor should the electronic collar be required with a youngster successfully trained to this standard.

The dummy launcher's real advantage is in sending the dummy a much greater distance than it is likely to be thrown by the trainer himself. An assistant suitably placed, as indicated, can always be as effective without the undesirable whip-crack of the blank. It must be admitted that at this stage, of course, an assistant with a dummy launcher can help the youngster to mark and retrieve at ever increasing ranges. On the other hand if the opportunity can be had to pick up at a driven shoot the youngster is likely to gain the same experience only on the real thing. By this time the gundog should be ready for just such a challenge.

Quite an important part of the advanced training may well be negative. Thus it is important to check the youngster from committing those silly mistakes which are so common in the first year and help it over them when, inevitably, they do arise. The pointing of larks, or the spot where birds have been recently flushed, are typical of an immature dog's mistakes. Such mistakes are readily made especially with grouse and, on the moor, or in the stubble, larks can be deceptive to young dogs. It is also important for the youngster to distinguish the 'heel scent' (i.e. where a bird, or beast, has come from, as opposed to where it is going) from the main scent. However, these are all mistakes for which the dog should at first only be reprimanded lightly. If it continues to make the same mistake it should be rebuked firmly, but the probability is that after a few mistakes it will not repeat the errors.

With a pointing dog it is also important to introduce it to the problem of too much scent. A field of roots close to a covert where pheasants are bred will often contain several hundred birds. If the roots are worked slowly down towards the end away from the cover, the dog will probably start freezing on point every second step. In such conditions an inexperienced youngster may lose its head and bounce forward flushing a cloud of pheasants in front of it. It may then go quite wild, 'losing its nose' completely (i.e. unable to scent anything) and simply rushing in circles dispersing birds right, left and centre. The first time such a situation looks like arising, however obedient the youngster may be in ordinary circumstances, it is advisable to slip on the lead and take it on carefully, if at all. The best thing to do in fact is to go away since it cannot be in the best interests of the ground to have the pheasants disturbed in this manner. If it is a shooting day then either they are soon to be driven, in which case they should not be disturbed, or if the gun is alone there are too many for a single gun to deal with effectively and they should be left for another day.

It will be appreciated that advanced training in certain aspects may take place over several years. It is not every gundog owner who is fortunate enough to have an opportunity of shooting through the game book at every type of game each season. Nor is it every owner who regularly flights duck, or geese, or shoots pigeons over decoys, or, for that matter, goes ferreting. In fact since driven shooting and ferreting, or wildfowling tend to be at opposite ends of the shooting scale the chances are quite good that few dogs will have the opportunity to cover the entire spectrum.

It is most likely in the average case that some aspects of shooting are only very occasionally practiced. It would, anyway, be extremely uncommon for anyone to shoot ptarmigan more than half a dozen times in the season, even in suitable ground. The same is true of capercailzie, which are, like ptarmigan, restricted to certain areas of Scotland. In any event the shooting man and his dog, especially the shooting man and his pointer-retriever, have a lot to learn from each other wherever and whenever they are shooting. In order to achieve perfect communication between themselves as a team working together, they must both be prepared to go on learning all the time. Each day out should bring something new for one, or other, or both of them.

ADVANCED TRAINING: OUTLINE OF POINTS:

July to August or September:

Some attempt should be made to work dog on grouse; perferably as pointer-retriever, but if necessary in only one or other role: Introduce to blackgame and snipe if possible and ptarmigan if any chance.

September to October:

Should now be worked on partridges on stubbles and in roots: Must learn to work different pace in roots: First woodcock is possible: Early practice on duck flighting into stubbles.

October to December:

Pheasants; both driven and walking up, along with partridges: Pigeon decoying: If any opportunity to shoot capercailzie it should be taken.

January to March:

First experience of wildfowling on saltings and foreshore: Introduction to first geese: Ferreting; introduction to ferrets: Back end hare shooting.

March to June:

Working with dummy: Refresher obedience training: Decoying pigeons: Rabbiting: Working tests: Preparation for field trials in following August.

8 Brace Training

The trainer who is accustomed to working one dog may well think this is simple enough and that two dogs will not be so very much more difficult. In some ways, of course, this is quite true, but in others it is decidedly far from the case. Training two dogs is not always easy going, even though the finished spectacle of two dogs quartering their ground faultlessly, each working independently of the other, as they cross in front of their trainer, each backing the other's point and honouring the flush of game, or dropping to shot, is undoubtedly an extremely attractive sight. There can, however, be numerous difficulties in their training which are not encountered with only one dog.

In addition, when the two dogs are finally working together the trainer will find that he has to keep his attention focused on them the whole time. While working one dog it is, as indicated, important to 'read' carefully his reactions to the ground, each check, or half point, each movement of the head, or tail, thus, with practice, gaining a good idea of what game lies on the ground ahead. While it may not be desirable for the trainer to let his attention wander occasionally while working one dog alone it is not likely to have any harmful effect, but when working two dogs together even a momentary lack of attention can lead to missing some factor which should have been noted. The trainer's attention must therefore be concentrated on them the whole time. There simply cannot be a moment's relaxation and the same applies later when out shooting over them. Trite though it may be, the fact is that like many other things in life a polished performance is not achieved without a good deal of work and experience, in this case on the part of both dogs and trainer.

When working a brace of dogs it is, on the whole, desirable that they should be a matching pair. Ideally they should be matched for size, for sex and for age. In one respect it is really best, however, if they are diametrically opposed to each other and that is in colour. Leaving aesthetic criteria aside, the reason for this is simply that, while it is difficult enough keeping control of one dog quartering the ground some forty yards (37 m) ahead and more to each side, when two dogs are working together the problem is more than doubled. There is also then the problem of distinguishing them from each other at a glance and, however well the trainer may know his dogs, when the two are more or less identical, this can become a very considerable problem. It is easy when they are some distance out to miss the fact that one is working less well than the other, or, even worse, to mistake the one that has been in error and to start mentally, or even vocally, admonishing the wrong dog. This in turn, of course, can lead to confusion in the dogs' minds. Hence it is preferable to have at least some points of easy contrast to distinguish the two dogs at a glance.

In practice the average owner of a well-matched working brace will have either bred them, or bought them from the same litter, unless they are mother and daughter, or father and son, as is also often quite common. The alternative, of course, is that they are from different bloodlines, when they may very easily develop into quite different beasts in temperament, in looks and in working ability, however similar they may have seemed as pups. This latter state of affairs is very likely to be the result if the two do not have at least some relationship to each other, although they may have been bought as apparently similar pups with a view to being trained up as an evenly matched brace of working dogs.

All this is still not to say that an unevenly matched pair working together, even where totally dissimilar in working abilities, may not complement each other and make up a harmonious partnership. One may be an excellent air scenter, the other stronger on ground scent, or one may be first rate on feather, while the other responds better on fur. Alternatively one may work better in cover, while the other is a better water dog. There are always bound to be some differences in the working abilities of any two dogs, even if they are only noticeable to the trainer, but on the whole too great a diversity, especially in working ability, is not usually a satisfactory arrangement. It is obviously much better when the two work together as a well-balanced team, each as competent as the other, but covering their ground separately and yet supporting each other when required.

The dam and daughter combination can be a good one, although, by the very nature of things the partnership is inevitably shorter than that of a pair of the same age. There is also always the danger of the dam's influence being too strong for her daughter with uneven results. The same is true, of course, of the father and son combination and in either jealousy can be troublesome. Where the brace, whether male or female, are from the same litter the results are likely to be most satisfactory, although there can always be difficulties when training them and jealousy again can be a problem. Kennel jealousy, however, is always likely to be a problem with more than one dog and as long as it is not allowed to affect their work unduly that is the main thing. It can even be used to good effect at times by the trainer when he is training them up to work together.

Assuming that the trainer is starting with two pups of the same sex from the same litter, matched as far as possible for size, the initial kennelling and acclimatisation problems are very much simpler since the two will keep each other company. From the start, however, it is essential not only to differentiate between the pups, but to ensure that they respond individually. Thus their names must obviously be very different and, more importantly, sound different. Egg and Ham, for instance, would do well, while Ham and Spam, or Egg and Meg, would lead to frightful confusion all round.

From the very first meal each should have a separate dish and each should be made to sit in front of it before being waved on to eat. Initially it might be easier to feed them separately until they have learned this lesson, although they should then still both be fed at the same time. Later when being fed together and both made to sit, one may be allowed forward to eat first, while the other is firmly held back by command, or signal, before being also waved forward. The two, however, should alternate fairly regularly as to which is first to eat. Any sign of over-eagerness should be promptly penalised by making that particular pup wait.

The trainer must never, above all, allow any sign of favouritism in his dealings with the pups, even if any preference begins to make itself felt for one or the other. Indeed if the trainer is foolish enough to allow a preference to develop it is essential then to lean over backwards to favour the other pup, or the trainer's attitude will soon be sensed and kennel jealousy will start to bedevil the training. Although most people are unaware of showing favouritism it is one of the principal sources of kennel jealousy and the trainer should do his best to avoid it.

It is easy enough for the trainer accustomed to only one dog to transgress unwittingly in this respect. Basically whenever one pup is rewarded with a pat and a few words of praise, the other should also be patted and spoken to as well to show that it has not been forgotten. Whenever one has a lesson in front of the other it is important that the positions are then reversed and that the second pup has its turn. Apart from the power of example on such occasions, any jealousy which might be aroused is thus used to act as a spur rather than allowed to fester.

This is one of the most obvious pitfalls of brace training, but it is not so easily avoided as might be thought. Scrupulous fairness at all times is essential or serious jealousy can be aroused. Alternatively the pup may turn sullen and withdrawn, showing a stubborn resistance to aspects of the training, or else a headstrong disobedience. Such reactions can prove very hard to overcome. If it becomes a serious problem it may be best for the trainer to part with the pup concerned and either find a replacement, or keep just the one. As with all failures in training it should be appreciated that it is not the dog's fault, but it is to be hoped that the trainer will manage to prevent such a situation developing.

When well-matched pups have been selected from the same litter, have been fetched from their kennels, their names decided on and successfully acclimatised, the next stage is their initial training. This is where, almost immediately, the trainer's work is doubled. To start with and usually for a month or so at least, it is essential to give each pup a separate training session each day.

This should entail at least one lesson lasting a quarter of an hour for each of them, preferably one after the other, so that their progress can be mentally compared. Of course, if time can be spared for two sessions, then each pup should have two, with, if possible, one in the morning and one in the afternoon, or evening, thus taking up a full hour of the trainer's time on training alone. However the lessons, like the trainer's time, should be evenly shared between both pups, or kennel jealousy will result.

When enforcing the pups' initial training it is, of course, essential to command them each in turn by name. The feeding bowl routine should be carried out every day with regular variations regarding which pup is made to sit and which is sent forward to eat first. Once they are both lead trained there is nothing to stop the trainer taking them both out together at heel. They should certainly by then be sharing regular brief exercise periods, primarily for play, with considerable benefit. Then it may well be that the trainer begins to appreciate that having two pups has some advantages over only one for, apart from being taught together, they will also play together and exercise each other. It is a matter for the trainer to decide, but it is still probably better at this stage to train them to 'Sit' and stay individually before taking them out for serious lessons together. Then, once again, each order must be addressed to them first by name, hence the importance of the feeding routine.

Once they have mastered the long drop they may certainly be taken out regularly on the lead at heel together and tested in turn, or together, to ensure that they are firmly grounded in this particularly important aspect of the initial obedience training. The trainer should soon find, when taking both pups out on the lead at heel, that letting one off at a time for a lesson proves a positive incentive to each of them for good behaviour. The desire to show off and the pressures of jealousy can work as powerfully on pups as on humans, so that each may do its best to outvie the other. The trainer should certainly use this as a spur to successful training, but, as already stressed, must also be careful to ensure even sharing between the pups, with equal time for training devoted to each of them, since they will be quick to notice and resent any unfairness in their treatment.

While the trainer with only one pup has plenty of time to study its temperament and work out the various reasons for its reactions to training, as well as the necessary counters, when it comes to taking on two pups the task is in many ways a much more complex one. The trainer then not only has to assess the character of each of the pups, their general temperament and their reactions to training, but also has to work out how much the one affects the other. The interaction of the two personalities, especially in relation to their trainer, is bound to raise problems, however friendly the pups may be with each other. Almost inevitably one pup will become the more dominant member of the pair, but this should never be allowed to get out of proportion. Where necessary the trainer can usually hold the balance to some extent and should endeavour to do so without allowing it to become obvious and raising the spectre of kennel jealousy.

Once the initial obedience training has been firmly inculcated into each pup it is up to the trainer to decide when to start either of them on retrieving, or pointing, training. Almost inevitably one of the pups will prove more forward than the other at retrieving and it may well be at pointing also, or alternatively each may be more forward than the other in one instinct, although if the trainer is lucky they may both come on at approximately the same pace. Here the advantage of having two pups training together is soon obvious in that any advances made by one are almost immediately likely to be copied by the other. It is very seldom, when the trainer has had both pups from the same age, that one lags for very long behind the other in developing its basic instincts. It has to be admitted, however, that when this does happen the trainer is liable to have considerable difficulty. On the other hand the chances are that this is one of those rare problems which if totally ignored will vanish of its own accord. The power of example and the spur of jealousy, as well as the desire to please, quite apart from the natural upsurge of instinct will usually have their combined effect.

The approach to retrieving must depend on the degree of instinct shown by the pups and the trainer's own decision. As with the training for the long drop it is probably desirable to start

each pup individually. Once they have mastered the initial retrieve the same routine may be followed, with each pup being
called in turn by name to execute a retrieve watched by the
other. The training should then carry on from there. Initially
when a dummy is marked only one pup at a time should be made
to mark it, but later, when each has proved itself capable of
retrieving in these circumstances, they can be made to mark
together. Subsequently, of course, only one can be sent to fetch
the dummy. The other must, however, then be allowed its turn
to make a similar retrieve, thus keeping the balance even
between them. The retrieving training therefore becomes a fairly
routine matter, following the general methods suggested, once
the trainer has mastered the principle of training two dogs instead
of one.

When it comes to more advanced retrieving the trainer has
only to continue in the same way. It is simply a question of
controlling the pups by name, command, signal and whistle in
turn. For instance two, three or more dummies may be thrown
round various points of the compass and the youngsters made to
mark them. Then each in turn may be sent to fetch one or other
of the marked dummies, with distractions such as the rolling
dummy, or thrown dummies, being encountered in the course
of the retrieve. Alternatively, of course, one pup may be sent to
fetch all the dummies, one after another, so long as the other is
then given a similar opportunity. Possibly, on the other hand,
the trainer may fetch all the dummies personally to enforce the
lesson that the youngsters are not always expected to retrieve.
Whereas the variations with one dog at this stage are considerable, when it comes to training two dogs the possibilities are
vastly increased. The trainer will also find it fascinating watching each pup's reactions to the various lessons.

Teaching the youngsters to hunt is best begun separately until
each pup is capable of quartering reasonably well. Once they
have begun to quarter their ground with some understanding of
what is required they may both be taken out together. They
should each be cast off in turn in opposite directions and then
worked by signal, command and whistle. If either shows any
inclination to shadow the other it must be dropped instantly and

the other waved on. As soon as they are separated the offender should be sent off firmly in the opposite direction. This should be repeated whenever either shows signs of failing to quarter independently, until they understand what is required.

Pointing is rather different, in that when one pup comes on point it is desirable for the other to honour the point. As with retrieving training it is up to the trainer to decide whether or not to start each pup individually in the initial stages, but if they are both reliable on the long drop it is not important to do so. One or both pups are likely to start by sight pointing in the manner indicated earlier and when one starts behaving in this way the chances are that the other will begin to follow its example.

Even where one pup shows no instinct to point the likelihood is that when the other has begun to point it will stiffen in a half-instinctive reaction to honour the point by backing. If it does not do so the trainer should make it 'Sit' at once, but even if there is initially no sign of backing there is no real need to worry as the instinct will manifest itself fairly soon. Should the need arise it is always possible to encourage the backward pup by bringing it up on a check lead as described with a pup and an older dog. When one pup starts pointing firmly this is almost certainly sufficient to bring on the second.

The stage has now been reached when some dizzied pigeons should be laid out in a field for the youngsters to find. They should then be quartered over the ground until one comes on point, whereupon, if it fails to honour the point by backing, the other must be promptly dropped, by whistle, command or signal. It should be made to remain in position until the bird is flushed and both dogs should then be dropped to flush. Until each learns to back properly and show no tendency to try to press forward to steal the other's point the trainer should always be ready to drop the youngster not on point. As with training a single dog the two must learn to hunt their ground, find their game, point, honour the point by backing, also acknowledge the flush and shot by dropping. The brace are in fact reaching the stage where they should be capable of working together in earnest.

Before being shot over together as a brace it is undoubtedly important to introduce the youngsters to the actual shooting individually. Although one may be kept at heel while the other is working the ground, it is only when they have each had their individual points shot over and their first retrieves in earnest that they should be worked together. When they are then worked as a brace it is always desirable to ensure that the dog which makes the point is awarded with the retrieve. As a general rule it is only when there are two retrieves to be made that the dog which failed to point should be allowed to retrieve a bird. If the dog which made the point is consistently refused the opportunity to retrieve it is very likely to become soured. This in turn might lead to refusal to point, or to back, or indeed to retrieve. In the circumstances these resistances are merely good examples of kennel jealousy.

The other important feature that the trainer must concentrate on at this stage is ensuring that the youngsters always work quite independently of each other. The worst fault of all is when one of a brace of dogs is seen to be following the other instead of each criss-crossing and working their ground separately. When one dog is seen to be shadowing another it invariably means that only one is really doing any work. The other is merely dogging its footsteps and allowing it to find the game. This may be because one dog is the more dominant character, but more probably it is the product of inefficient training. Once established this pattern is not an easy one to alter.

Advanced dependence of this nature by one dog of a brace on the other is most often seen when a young dog is set to work with an older beast which has thoroughly dominated it, but clearly it should never be tolerated in any circumstances. On the other hand, inevitably, as a brace come to work for any length of time together one or other will tend to leave certain aspects of work to its partner to tackle if it is allowed to get away with it. Shirking of this kind should always be checked whenever spotted by the trainer, but it is not always the easiest of things to mark.

It may well be, for example, that one dog of a brace is keener on entering cover than the other. In that case it may well be noticed, if they are carefully watched, that while one dog is thrusting directly into cover the other is only entering the outside, although giving an appearance of willingness. The same may be true of water, where one dog may be a better swimmer than the other and accordingly gets left the stickier retrieves, although its partner may assist in a small way by marking the game and even directing the other to it.

When quartering their ground it is always as well to keep a mental tally of the number of points made by each dog. If the majority of points are always being made by one dog it may well indicate that the other is happy merely to coast along leaving most of the work to its partner. The dog may, of course, be off colour, or this may be an example of the sort of resistance attributable to kennel jealousy, which was mentioned earlier. It might be that the dog is feeling in some way jealous and is simply not trying any longer. This may have been caused by the trainer seeming to favour the other dog in some way without anticipating the result of his action. Whatever the reason it should certainly be stopped before it becomes a habit.

In any such case the answer, of course, is to separate the dogs temporarily and work them apart. With one dog at heel and the other working there is no excuse for this sort of behaviour and whenever anything of this nature is noticed the dog concerned should be severely castigated verbally and immediately put to work by itself, or, if this is to its taste, perhaps made to stay at heel. The trainer should always try to make the punishment suit the crime and when suitably punished dogs can feel every bit as ashamed as humans.

So far reference has mainly been to two pups evenly matched and growing up as a matched pair. This is not, of course, always the case, even with pups chosen from the same litter and sometimes one pup will develop into a long-legged loping dog, while the other is a smaller, faster moving animal. Misfits of this nature intended as working partners are generally the result of pups taken from different litters, but sometimes even from the same litter differences in temperament and instinct, as much as size, can be very unfortunate to put it mildly.

Extreme differences in size and temperament in a working brace are obviously undesirable and inevitably result in indifferent quartering, if nothing else, since one will be moving faster than the other. It is difficult to control this except by trying to work them so that one has a shorter beat than the other, only slightly overlapping. Compromises of this sort are unfortunate, but if you are trying to work an unevenly matched pair together they are probably inevitable. If the dogs are not compatible temperamentally this can be even worse. This will generally become plain during the training as the pups are growing up together. Unfortunately matters may well have reached quite an advanced stage before it is fully appreciated that the dogs cannot work together for one reason or another, as for instance advanced kennel jealousy, and the only solution is to part with one of them.

When working an older dog with a younger one, such as dam and daughter, or sire and son, the important point is always to train and work the youngster entirely by itself as far as possible in the first instance. It may be useful to use the older dog occasionally to emphasise an aspect of the training and to show the youngster what is required. This is something, however, that should never be overdone. It is especially not desirable to lead the youngster around behind the older dog on a check lead to teach it to point, if they are subsequently to work together, since this may well lead to blinking (i.e. failure to point, or not remaining staunch on point). If the example of the older dog is used, however, with the youngster running free, as with the two pups together, this should be all right. It is however very easy for the older dog to dominate the youngster. As indicated this can lead to the younger dog merely shadowing the older one and having no initiative of its own.

Although an older dog should never be allowed to dominate a younger one, especially during training, there are always exceptions in such matters. Where a gentle dam and forward daughter are concerned, for instance, or a mild mannered sire and aggressive son, it may well be that the power of example can be very useful in training and there would be little danger of undue domination by the older animal. Teaching the meaning of the various whistles, signals and commands for initial obedience may then be done partially, at least, by example. Retrieving and pointing may also be taught in the same way with the older animal showing the youngster what is required.

With a suitable mentor and pupil this can sometimes prove a very painless method of training, but again it should never be overdone. The youngster should always be made to work on its own for a good part of its training, if only to prove that it is capable of working by itself and to encourage it to use its initiative. Thereafter the youngster may well work perfectly well with its mentor. A great deal will always depend on the individual dogs as well as the way they are handled and trained.

In training, the pairing of opposites can sometimes be useful. This is especially the case where a dog has apparently developed a resistance to some aspect of work. Paired with a dog which excels in this particular field the power of example may well prove sufficient. The good retriever fetching the dummy may inspire the dog which has obstinately refused to do so. If as a last resort they are coupled together with a quite short linkage between their collars this may also prove surprisingly effective in some cases.

When the doctor, already mentioned in previous chapters, finally returned the youngster I had trained for him it proved to be as I had expected quite remarkably wild. All its training had been forgotten and if it saw anything moving at the far end of a thirty acre (12 ha) field it would attempt to take off for it and, since it was by then a large and powerful animal, this proved something of a trial. Soon after its arrival an old friend sent me a dog which matched it for size, although extremely fat and supposedly gun-shy. Since I knew this dog's breeding and was convinced it was merely gun nervous I had agreed to take it and see what I could do with it. This was a very different phenomenon in that I had to drag it round the shoot on a rope lashed to my waist. The first day I must have walked the best part of ten miles (16 km) in this fashion tugging that dog all the way before it struck me that I had two opposites on my hands.

The next day I took the so-called gun-shy dog out coupled firmly to the dog which had returned from the doctor with a rope attached to the couple and more or less let them get on with it. It was not a case of 'Those in front cried back and those behind cried forward'. It was more a case of 'He in front cried forward and he behind cried back', but both being large and determined they more or less cancelled each other out. By the end of the day they were both behaving comparatively sensibly. It was only after a few days when the so-called gun-shy dog started taking an interest in the proceedings and charging forward together with his companion that I was forced to end the situation. They had, however, both learned something from the experiment. From that stage onwards their cures both began to take effect.

When two shooting men are out with their pointer-retrievers in the field there are often very ill-assorted couples set to work together. It is, of course, impossible to improve on Nature. A small out-at-elbows dog cannot be expected to cover the ground as smoothly and effortlessly as a well-made, well-built animal. A dog with no natural nose cannot be expected to point, or retrieve, as well as a dog with fine scenting abilities. There is absolutely no point in partnering a large, young, fast moving specimen with a small and pottery old dog on a moor. The best plan in such circumstances is to work only one dog and keep the other at heel, possibly allowing it to assist when it comes to retrieving. It should be remembered, however, that just as a youngster can be taught correct behaviour by the example of a well trained dog, it can, even more quickly, learn bad habits from the example set by disobedient animals in the shooting field.

Bracework has many pitfalls for the unwary. On the other hand the sight of a well-matched, well-balanced pair of dogs working their ground in unison, criss-crossing each other, then coming on point and backing each other instantly like a pair of statues is a splendid spectacle. When the dogs then drop to flush and shot and each may be sent either simultaneously, or separately, to retrieve their birds, it is a sight to gladden the heart of any owner. If they have been trained and worked by the owner-breeder there can be few more completely satisfying moments in the shooting field.

9 Training the Mature Dog

Unfortunately it is seldom that a trainer has the chance of taking on a mature dog, of say eighteen months to two years, or more, which has not already developed a number of faults and resistances to training. An unspoiled dog of over two years is a rarity. Either it has received absolutely no training, in which case it is probably as wild as a hawk, not even answering to its name, or it may be fat and spoiled, reluctant to obey any commands, reluctant even to follow its natural instincts. Alternatively the dog's natural instincts may have become warped. It may have learned to chase and kill rabbits, to run in on birds and even to chase them too. There are, unfortunately, remarkably few dogs of this sort of age which have not been spoiled almost beyond redemption, in one way or another.

On the other hand there are few trainers who would not willingly take a dog of mature age, if they could be guaranteed that it was receptive to training and had not been spoiled. It is then really a much easier animal to train than a young pup, where the training, because of the youngster's age, has to be spread over six to nine months, or even longer. With a mature animal the training can be speeded up and should take no more than three months or so at the most. This, of course, has its pitfalls too, since there is not the same time as there is with a pup to instil absolutely firmly the initial obedience training which is such an essential foundation for the whole training edifice. While many trainers might like to keep a dog until a mature age for training, it is extremely hard to do so unspoiled in some way and probably not advisable to try, but better, as indicated, to channel the instincts as they develop.

The principle difference between a mature dog and a puppy when it comes to training is that the trainer can not only afford to take a firmer line with it, but is almost certainly forced to do so. Whereas a pup can be effectively punished simply by using a firm tone when admonishing it, the mature dog may need more active discouragement. Even so it is never desirable to use physical force if it can possibly be avoided. The best punishment for a dog of any age is a firm shaking, lifting it by the scruff of the neck and loose skin of the back, or alternatively chastising it by biting the ear in the manner of the leader of the pack.

It is as well, however, to take certain precautions with a mature dog. For instance one owner to whom I recommended this procedure tried it and was astounded to find the results were excellent. The next time, however, when attempting to repeat this form of chastisement, the dog was aware of what to expect. It very sensibly showed that it had learned its lesson by getting its bite in first and leaving the would-be trainer with a set of teethmarks on the nose. When chastising in this manner therefore it is advisable to hold the dog so that it cannot respond in kind. The aim and object of the punishment in any event is not so much to emphasise that the dog has transgressed but also to show it that the leader of the pack objects to such behaviour.

As with a puppy the aim of the trainer should be to persuade the dog to behave in the manner desired, to channel its natural instincts, and achieve a working relationship by always keeping a few steps ahead of it in any situation. In order to do so, of course, the trainer should know in advance the likely reactions to training and the appropriate counters. Fortunately, on the whole, almost any dog's reactions are likely to be fairly predictable. It is in knowing how and when to apply the appropriate counters that the trainer's skill is fully exercised.

With a mature dog the initial training should not be necessary. It should know its name and respond to various words of command. It should come when called, to command, whistle and signal. It is to be hoped that it has been taught to sit, or drop, when given the appropriate command, signal, or whistle. With good fortune it has also been taught the long drop. That is the ideal, but this may be hoping for too much and there is always the possibility that it does not even know its name.

Where the trainer has to start completely from scratch, with a dog refusing even to acknowledge its name, or respond to any command, it is probably wise to refuse to have anything to do with it since the likelihood is that it has developed so many resistances to training through mishandling that it is past redemption. If, however, the trainer is determined to persevere it will be necessary to take certain precautions.

The initial training in such a case is best conducted in an enclosed yard, or similar space, where the dog cannot distance itself at will from the trainer. The only problem here may be that the dog will behave perfectly when thus restricted and in the open, aware of its advantage, will pay no attention whatsoever to the trainer. In such cases a check cord is worth trying in the first instance, but again the likelihood is that the mature dog, which has been allowed to have its own way, will behave perfectly with a check cord on, but as soon as it is removed will go its own way. Furthermore a check cord needed to hold a mature dog of say fifty pounds (22.7 kg) or more will have to be quite a stout rope. The problem is not insoluble, but it is likely to take time. A shortcut, in such circumstances, is to use an electronic collar, but that will be dealt with in greater detail later.

In such a case it may be necessary to enforce the initial training within an enclosed space only and go on quickly to encourage the pointing and retrieving instincts. If these instincts have not been spoiled the problem becomes immediately much simpler. Once the dog has been encouraged to point and can be relied on to remain staunch it is possible to set out dizzied pigeons and gradually gain control over it. When the dog is also prepared to retrieve, the training is again much easier. In such a case it may well be politic to enforce the obedience training by means of the pointing and retrieving lessons.

With any mature dog, especially one which has been allowed to develop bad habits, or where the instincts have been to some degree warped, it may be sensible to scrap the ordinary training programme and work as the dog's reactions decree. The important point is always to gain control by one means or another. If the dog reacts well to retrieving then a start with the retrieving training may prove the right answer. If it reacts more obviously to the pointing instinct this is probably the place to start. The main thing is to establish a link with the dog and obtain a response from it.

Once any communication has been established the trainer should go on from there and build up an ever increasing area of control. Any preconceived ideas about how the dog should be trained will have to be discarded and the system simply geared to the dog's reactions. It is in fact up to the dog to show how its training should be conducted, in that the trainer must simply respond to any sign of interest and work on from there. By degrees the area of control will be steadily widened and communication between dog and trainer gradually increased.

In such cases, where it is essential first to establish a degree of communication with the dog, rather than follow any preconceived training schedule, it may even be desirable to start by shooting over the dog and working back to training with the dummy or dizzied pigeons. From there it should be possible to work back to initial obedience training, thus conducting the training schedule in reverse. In effect there is absolutely no stage in the training schedule which may not have to be used as a starting point with a mature dog that has been thoroughly spoiled when a youngster. As indicated the first essential is to establish communication with it and if the only way to do so is to encourage its instinct by, for instance, shooting a rabbit in front of it, then that may well be the best way to start.

In practice the dog which has been allowed to roam wild and out of control may sometimes be preferable to the wretched animal which has been kept indoors, in an enclosed kennel, and never allowed out so that it is nervous of every sight and sound. Such a dog may well be classified as gun-shy, but, as indicated earlier, truly gun-shy dogs are a rarity and it is very much more probable that it is merely gun nervous. A neurotic psychological case of this nature may, however, prove extremely difficult to cure.

The symptoms of gun-nervousness, or for that matter gun-shyness, are quite impressive. At the sight of a gun the dog may immediately run away and hide, or, if restrained, try to fight to get away, roll over on its back, or bury its head under cover. When restrained on the lead its contortions may be very violent, to the degree of nearly strangling itself. The sound of a shot in the distance will send it quivering into a corner, or into shelter, under a table, or somewhere similar. The average reaction usually is that such a dog cannot possibly ever be expected to work in the field. While this reaction is quite understandable it is usually quite wrong.

The dog mentioned in the previous chapter appeared to be a classic case, although in fact it had been trained to the gun and then later developed this inexplicable gun-shyness, or, more properly, gun-nervousness. Its owner, an old friend, had despaired of it, but as I knew its breeding I agreed to take it. While doing its best to refuse to accompany me, even to the extent of being dragged several yards lying twisting and struggling on its back, this dog never gave up an active resistance throughout most of the first day's shooting, although eventually walking reluctantly and sullenly at heel when it found there was no alternative.

After three days of being hauled round in my company coupled to the dog returned from the doctor and being regularly shot over, there came the moment when it moved tentatively of its own accord towards a shot rabbit rolling backwards down a slope towards it. From then onwards, with its dormant hunting instinct aroused again, its cure began and it progressed rapidly. All fear of the gun, pretended or real, vanished completely. After that it was a straightforward and comparatively simple re-training exercise.

Visiting my friend's house to see if I could find how the problem had originated I discovered, after a little detective work, that the butler was in the habit of keeping a bowl of food always ready and waiting under the kitchen table for the dog. It was here the animal retired whenever it saw a gun. In the choice between work and food the latter had, very understandably perhaps, proved more tempting and the dog had then developed this psychological neurosis at the sight or sound of the gun. It was a situation which was easily remedied and merely required a stern word with the butler. Thereafter the problem remained solved.

Another very similar example was that of a bitch of my own

breeding. This had gone to some people I knew well, but from the start matters went awry. The journey by train in the travelling kennel was very long and must have had its effect for when the pup was finally released at its new home it bolted down a cellar drain and was only extracted with great difficulty. This was, of course, not its fault. Thereafter it was introduced to the gun by being shot over with a .22 rifle and predictably was again frightened. The new owner then proclaimed that it was a pleasant dog, but gun-shy, and did not attempt to train it.

After visiting him, when incidentally I saw it pointing on its own and being backed by two miniature dachshunds, I was certain that it was not gun-shy, offering to take it back and train it as proof. However it was retained as a family pet despite my protests that this was a waste of a good dog. Then finally they moved house and at my suggestion it went to an acquaintance of mine who wished to start a kennel, as it was by then four years old and a suitable foundation bitch for him.

The new owner then agreed to let me have the bitch to see if I could cure it of this supposed gun-shyness. Since it was gentle and nothing like as large as the dog mentioned previously I had little trouble in taking the bitch round with me and by the second day it was over the neurosis and its hunting instincts were aroused. Within a week I was shooting over it and within a fortnight it was showing all the makings of a surprisingly good working dog considering its background and the short time that had been spent on its training. The new owner shot over it with me and then took it back with him. Despite my warnings to take matters gently, he then at once took it out on a full scale driven shoot and claimed that it reverted to neurosis again. He then bred from it regularly so that it never had a further chance to work. The moral, I suppose, is that dogs may be trainable at any stage but some people never are.

The problems which arise with mature dogs are generally deep seated neuroses, such as gun-nervousness, rather than intrinsic faults. Thus a common failing quite often seen is a refusal to retrieve to hand, dropping the fur, or feather, or for that matter the dummy, several feet away. This is almost always because at some point the dog has been scolded, or even chastised, for something when bringing a retrieve to hand. It may have been retrieving something like a prized doll, or a crocodile skin handbag, or it may simply have run in to shot and fall of game and been reprimanded for that on its return with the retrieve, naturally associating the harsh words with the retrieve and not the running in.

The solution to this has already been indicated in the chapter on retrieving. Initially the trainer should try to cure it by running away as the dog comes with the retrieve and continue running until the dog is alongside him. Then it should be encouraged verbally and finally the retrieve accepted, if necessary on the move. If this is successful all is easy, as it is merely a question of progressing on from there. It may, however, not be quite so simple.

If the dog still persists in putting the retrieve down at a distance, it should be worth tying the dummy in its jaws with a loop round the back of the head as outlined earlier. After initial efforts to reject it, when its reactions may be as frenzied as those of the gun nervous dog, the dummy should be accepted and the dog should soon start to wave its tail. Once the dog has accepted the principle of carrying the dummy in the vicinity of the trainer the resistance is virtually overcome. Thereafter the reaction of putting down the retrieve before it is told to should not arise. It should, however, be emphasised that when the dog performs successfully in a case such as this it should be praised verbally and at length. It should also be soothed verbally and if necessary physically throughout, for in such cases the human voice properly applied is amongst the trainer's most valuable assets.

A persistent and firm refusal to retrieve may have its roots in some similar puppyhood incident which remains firmly in the dog's mind causing a total block. The same method, indicated above, of tying the dummy in the dog's mouth may well prove effective. Once the refusal to pick up and carry has been mastered the training can continue from there. When the cause has been removed the problem usually ceases to exist. Normal methods of training can then be resumed if they are any longer required, but the chances are that once the mental block is removed all will be well.

Where the dog persistently picks up the retrieve and shakes it or, worse still, crunches it, or even eats it, the average reaction is that the dog has hard mouth and is unusable as a retriever. Of course, it is highly desirable that from the first moment any such behaviour is noted the dog is taken in hand at once. Such reactions are usually begun as a pup and may be caused initially by high spirits, but more frequently are the result of boredom. Repeated repetition of the same sort of retrieve may well cause the young dog to shake the dummy in pure frustration. From that stage on the training may have gone from bad to worse.

If, however, any dog persists in closing the suitcase on game retrieves, flattening them so that all the ribs are broken and they are virtually uneatable, it is worse than useless as a retriever. It follows that strong measures may be taken without fear of making the situation any worse. Whether the advanced cases of hard mouth can ever be cured effectively once they have become ingrained is very much open to question, but it is what might be termed a no-holds-barred situation, as are most failures of training in the mature dog. It is therefore worth trying everything possible.

Initially the same policy of tying the dummy in the jaws may be tried. Where the dog has developed the habit of 'closing the suitcase' (i.e. closing its jaws on the retrieve)' this may well not prove a cure. The dummy may be carried, but be thoroughly chewed. The problem here is to persuade the dog to carry the retrieve gently without force. The old remedy used to be to encourage them to retrieve a hedgehog and there are modern equivalents. A rubber core dummy with barbed wire rolled round it and a thin canvas covering·so that if the dog closes its jaws it is going to receive a sharp pain is a possible solution, but care must be taken to use this judiciously so that it does not learn that only one particular dummy has teeth. Anyway this may still not affect its game retrieving.

If the barbed wire dummy has failed, really desperate measures are called for and it may be worth trying a variant on forced retrieving. The advocates of forced retrieving say that a dog should be taught to retrieve by placing the bird, or dummy, in its jaws and at any attempt to spit it out the ear should be nipped painfully. This should be repeated every time the dog tries to get rid of the dummy but as soon as it carries it correctly the ear should be released so that the pain ceases. The dog thus comes to appreciate that if it does not carry the dummy it is likely to suffer pain. If this process is accompanied by appropriate verbal praise, or threat and prohibition, the chances are that the trainer's voice by itself might be sufficient.

In any event, it might be worth practicing a variant of this method on the dog. This would entail first tying a bird, such as a crow, in the dog's jaws. Whenever the dog showed signs of trying to spit it out, or close the suitcase, the ear should be nipped with a firm verbal prohibition. When it carries it correctly with no attempt to close the suitcase, or chew, the dog should, of course, be praised and the ear released. There is always a chance this might be successful, but every dog will react individually.

It is, of course, always helpful to know the basic cause of any such resistance as those described, As indicated it may well all have started with boredom, but it may have been, for instance, that when still a youngster and on one of its early live retrieves it was scratched by the spurs of an old cock pheasant, or pecked by a crow. An attempt by a youngster to deal with a hare not cleanly killed and still struggling violently can also be a common cause of incipient hard mouth. Some such cause could either result in failure to retrieve at all, or alternatively, with some dogs, a tendency to get its own back, and assert itself, or prevent a repetition, by ensuring that the game is thoroughly dead when it is finally retrieved to hand. It is always important to look at the possible results of any actions while the pup is still maturing.

Where the dog persistently runs in to shot, or fall of game, all that is usually required is for the trainer to abstain from shooting and allow someone else to do so while standing over it and ensuring that it does not transgress. The same process is usually sufficient to prevent the dog giving chase after hares and rabbits, if it shows a tendency to do so. When the dog comes on point on ground game it is only necessary to abstain from shooting and ensure that the dog is firmly restrained by verbal and if necessary physical action. This, of course, is always assuming that the dog has been properly trained in the first place. Where the dog has never been prevented from giving chase, or where the habit has become ingrained, simply through idleness on the trainer's part, it becomes more difficult. A check lead will probably not be any use since the mature dog is usually aware of the meaning of such a lead and will not transgress when it is in place.

There are, naturally, a number of vices, which are not uncommon in mature dogs that have not yet been mentioned. Self-hunting, when the dog takes to going off hunting on its own, or with a companion, is a very tiresome vice. It also indicates a certain degree of carelessness on the trainer's part in that the dog, or dogs, have to have the opportunity to get loose on their own. If they are properly supervised in a well organised enclosed kennel yard such a vice is unlikely to arise. With bitches in season, however, or dogs inspired by the mating instinct, kennel security has to be thoroughly sound for one lapse can lead to a dog, or bitch going astray. Once the vice is started it is extremely hard to cure. Like most other such vices prevention is the best and soundest cure.

Where there is even a possibility of such a wandering dog chasing sheep, of course, the situation is desperate and it is esential to do everything possible to prevent it. Sheep chasing may start quite innocently with a pup merely wishing to play. It must, of course, be curbed at all costs. One method of dealing with it is to hold any offending dog in a pen with an old black-faced ewe with a lamb at foot. The ewe with its curving horns will butt the wretched dog until it never wishes to see a sheep again.

When the doctor's dog first returned to me it took off on the first day and went through a field of sheep, paying little attention to them, although it did roll one over. Fortunately I was not far behind it and at the sight and sound of my approach it ran on with barely a check. I went back intending to get out the gun to shoot it, but, fortunately for it, the dog had returned home before me. Then I applied this drastic remedy, allowing the ewe to butt it unmercifully, and to my knowledge it never looked at a sheep again. The drawback to this cure, of course, is that not everyone has blackfaced ewes available to hand.

This is one occasion, as is the complete refusal to answer to name or any command, when an electronic collar is probably worth its very considerable cost as an aid to training. The ability to give a dog a very effective electric jolt at a distance of a quarter of a mile (.4 km) or more can, on occasions, be very useful. On the other hand these devices, to my mind, have very considerable and grave shortcomings which do not make them necessarily the answer to the novice trainer's prayer. They can in my view be very harmful unless used with great care.

Electronic collars can be had in varying degrees of sophistication and at very widely differing cost. The basic model is little more than a receiving device attached to the collar which will automatically give the dog an electric shock within a given distance when the trainer presses a button on a sending device. The most sophisticated models will carry a long distance, will provide various degrees of shock if required and will also, either at the same time, or separately, give a warning bleep, or buzz. Thus the dog can be given a warning bleep prior to receiving a shock.

This, of course, is a useful training technique and if one could be sure of utter reliability it could be extremely useful. On the other hand, even with transistors and today's advanced electronic technology, the receiver on the collar is quite bulky and it would not be desirable to work a dog with this comparatively heavy lump protruding from its collar. While permissible, even in some circumstances useful, for certain sorts of training, it is, however, not really to be recommended for work. This, therefore, to a large extent negates the possible advantage of being able to train the dogs to bleeps on the receiver rather than whistles. Like many another aspect of training it is best in the long run to keep everything as simple as possible.

Some fifteen years ago I had one of the latest models of electronic dog collars then manufactured in the U.S.A. This consisted of a sender, with extendable aerial, and the receiver fitted to the dog's collar, with two studs protruding through it. These gave the dog a shock at a distance of up to half a mile (.8 km) when the button on the sender was pressed. Two degrees of shock could be given, either mild, or more severe. At that stage, even in these most expensive models, they were not wired for sound. No doubt the models today are also less bulky, but even so I doubt if the major snag has yet been overcome.

The trouble is that there is always the danger of interference with such devices, depending, as they do on contact via the air waves. Just as so many model aircraft have suddenly gone out of control due to interference from some other sending device so these cannot possibly be guaranteed against the dog receiving either a bleep, or, worse still, a shock of varying strength at the wrong moment. While it might conceivably be worth risking this to use them briefly to attempt to cure a rogue sheep chaser, or a dog gone completely wild and refusing to answer to any other control, their continuous use could not be recommended.

My own electronic dog collar was purloined some ten years or more ago by a technical electronics specialist officer in the Royal Navy. Although I was extremely annoyed at the time, it says a great deal about them that I have seldom felt any real regrets, or any desire to acquire another. As indicated, they have their uses, but these are distinctly limited and on the whole they are not devices which should generally be used by novice trainers. Even used with care they could quite easily work incorrectly at an important moment and thus to a large extent prove of negative value.

Taken all in all the novice trainer would be best advised not to take on a mature dog unless he knows its general background and feels there is a strong likelihood of its training being successful. Where the dog has a sullen demeanour and is slow to approach the trainer when called, or stands off at a distance nervously, or suspiciously, it is very obvious that it has been mishandled. However sorry one may feel for such an animal, and it is certainly not its fault, the problems likely to be encountered in training are such that it is definitely best to leave it alone. While it might in time, with attention and care, make a likeable pet, or if a good specimen, even a winning show dog, it will not easily make a working dog.

The other kind of dog which it is usually best to avoid, although this might not at once be apparent, is the dog which bounces forward in a friendly manner, barking or whining, leaping up irrepressibly on everyone who approaches it, obviously full of life and energy. Although apparently very friendly and engaging, such a dog may not even recognise its own name. The probability is that it has been allowed to run wild and has in consequence developed all sorts of vices which may prove almost impossible to eradicate. There is no point in the trainer taking on someone else's liabilities, however outwardly attractive the dog may be.

The most important feature in a mature dog undoubtedly is its temperament, which is much more easily judged than that of a six to eight week old pup. If the dog approaches willingly and fearlessly waving its tail quietly it almost certainly has an amiable nature and is willing to please. Such a dog is likely to be comparatively straightforward when it comes to training, although there may always be hang-ups of one sort or another caused by previous mishandling. Given a good temperament to start with and once communication has been established satisfactorily the chances are that dog and trainer will form a sound working partnership.

If the novice trainer does decide to take on a mature dog, having first investigated its background as far as possible, there are certain advantages to be gained by doing so. The trainer can expect to conclude the training within three months or so, as opposed to a year or eighteen months, although, of course, both dog and trainer must then continue to broaden their mutual experience together. The trainer must, however, be prepared to work alongside the dog and learn at times from it. This can on occasions prove a singularly rewarding and exciting experience, but the same is true of many aspects of gundog training, especially when covering the whole gamut of work with a pointer-retriever.

10   Tests, Trials and Shooting Days

The average person having successfully trained a dog for the first time will probably wish to see how it compares with others. While to some extent this may be done in the shooting field the opportunities for comparison there are somewhat limited. No-one who enters the shooting field in a competitive frame of mind, either as regards shooting, or as regards working a dog, is likely to be very welcome. There are few things more irritating than this sort of attitude in what should be a relaxed and informal day amongst friends. If the owner has been attending training classes organised by some society, of course, there will have been numerous occasions to match the progress of the dog against the others in the class. In such a case, moreover, almost certainly the trainer and dog will be encouraged to enter a working test run by the society when the training season has been concluded. This is the usual way in which people, however non-competitive minded they may be, find themselves engaged in entering working tests, or possibly later field trials as well, and competing strenuously with their dogs.

Working tests for pointer-retrievers tend to be more difficult to organise than similar tests of specialist retrievers since it is, naturally, desirable to test not only their quartering and hunting, but also their pointing, abilities. This, of necessity, requires more room than can frequently be provided, for inevitably if dogs are worked over the same ground covered previously by other dogs and handlers, to test their ability to quarter, hunt and point game, the later entries will find the ground fouled by the first runners and the test must lack any degree of fairness. It is thus more common for such working tests only to cover their retrieving abilities, which is, of course, a great pity since this is only half of their working role.

While organising training classes for pointer-retrievers in the north some years back we developed a method of running a working test which does at least after a fashion simulate the real thing. If it is intended to test say ten dogs at quartering, hunting and pointing, it is feasible to set up a test of this kind given suitable ground. The absolute basic minimum required for each dog would be something in the region of two to three hundred yards (183–274 m) long into the wind, by one hundred yards (91 m) across. Somewhere between fifty and a hundred acres (20–40 ha) is about the minimum suitable area, but probably nearer the latter since much has to depend on the ground cover and such matters as the shape of fields and so on. The more ground available, of course, the better. It is, on the whole, preferable that this is not good farming land. Much better would be a hundred (40 ha) or more acres of some tussocky land with a few gorse bushes here and there.

Moving in from the direction of the prevailing wind the organisers should then lay one or more pigeons in cages on the ground chosen for each competitor. The reason for choosing cages, despite the interference with scent involved, is that this is probably the best method of laying a bird down well in advance and ensuring that it is still there when required. Thus the ground can be prepared the day before the event, but a map should be made of where the birds are laid out otherwise they can easily be missed.

Simply constructed wire netting cages without bottoms, which just stand on the ground are probably best, pegged at one side if necessary. If a long piece of fishing line is attached to the top leading to a suitable hazel wand marker, the organiser can be ready to pull the line and release the bird when the dog has pointed. It is thus possible to arrange for a bird to be flushed and a shot fired when each dog has come on point. At this stage an assistant should be ready to throw a dead bird from one or other end of the line and the dog may then be sent for a retrieve. By thus using a minimum of two helpers it is possible to test the quartering, hunting, pointing and retrieving roles, and simulate something close to the real thing.

In theory, of course, it should be possible in this fashion to simulate an entire pointer-retriever field trial, but it would require considerable land and a large number of helpers. There would also be very little point in doing so since if the land was available it would be more to the point to run a proper field trial on it, although possibly where there was no game available it might be justified. From my own experience, however, I have to admit that there are liable to be numerous snags, such as the wind changing abruptly overnight so that all the birds are set out in the wrong places with the lines in the wrong direction, or a fox, mink, or merely a wandering dog, may have upset many of the cages in an attempt to get at the occupants. To some extent, of course, these are the hazards facing any field trial organiser, for sudden weather changes, or the depredations of predators, or poachers, may have disastrous results on any such events, as anyone who has ever been involved with them will know only too well.

The number of entries in a working test such as that described is largely limited by the amount of ground available and the time for preparation. In full scale pointer-retriever field trials, as run in the U.K., the number of dogs run is limited to twelve since it has been found that this is about the limit that can be adequately tested in a day in normal circumstances, if they are to be worked in the open, in cover and in water, quartering their ground and hunting and pointing, as well as retrieving. It would probably be possible to raise the number of entries for a working test of this nature, since naturally it is much more limited as regards the extent to which the work can be judged when compared with a field trial on wild birds. Such a test is useful, to test young novice dogs that have successfully completed a training class over a period of months and are now ready for the field.

Much more common, because so much easier to organise, are working tests similar to those used for retrievers, although usually with variations. Working tests intended solely for retrievers have the advantage that they require much less ground. They can usually be conducted comfortably on ten acres (4 ha) of suitable ground, or quite possibly even less. In such working tests, for retrievers only, the dogs are walked at heel and a number of dummies have to be retrieved in succession. The degree of difficulty involved in each retrieve is usually progressive. Thus the first retrieve might be a straightforward one with a shot fired and a dummy thrown in full view. The second retrieve might be with the dummy thrown over a fence, hedge, dyke, or similar obstacle and the next retrieve might be unseen. The following retrieve might be on two dummies, one seen and one unseen, with the unseen one to be retrieved first; or there might be distractions such as another dummy thrown, or a rolling dummy bowled past the dog, and so on.

For the pointer-retriever variant of such working tests it is really desirable to have more ground, probably as much as twenty acres (8 ha). The reason for this is simply that it is preferable to have each dog quartering the ground some distance from its handler when the shot is fired and the dummy, or dead bird, is thrown. Otherwise the principle remains very much the same, with preferably one retrieve from cover and another from, or across, water thus proving that the dog is prepared to enter cover and can swim, as required in the field trial schedule. Such tests are several degrees more difficult than when the dog is at heel, but that, after all, is how the pointer-retriever is expected to work. Since these tests are easier to organise than the ones previously described the number of dogs that can be tested is likely to be nearly double. It is always important, however, when organising any such tests to work out the approximate time each retrieve takes and calculate the number of entries accordingly.

In any such working test the degree to which the real work in the field can be simulated is of course limited. On the other hand it is obviously desirable to make them as realistic as possible. For this reason it is probably preferable to use dead pigeons, rather than dummies, if sufficient can be obtained. No bird however should be used for more than one retrieve, because some dogs may refuse to retrieve game already retrieved by another, or else will mouth it. This means it is necessary to have access to a plentiful supply of pigeons, hence why dummies are more commonly used. It ought not to be beyond the bounds of possibility, however, to obtain some hundred and fifty dead pigeons, which would be sufficient for a twenty-five dog test. This is simply a matter of organisation.

To keep these tests as realistic as possible it is also desirable that the dummies, or birds, should be thrown by the assistants from concealed positions. If necessary a hide should be constructed for the purpose. It is also important to take the prevailing wind into account when organising such tests since this will have a considerable bearing on matters. When an assistant is sitting with a sack of pigeons up wind of the dogs it is more than likely that dog after dog will run straight to the sack, which, if nothing else, makes judging somewhat difficult.

To complete the picture and give the dog at least the impression of working in the field, one, or two, guns should walk with, or on either side of, the handler. They should be briefed, so that when a dummy, or bird, is thrown, they fire in approximately the correct direction. The dog will be cast off by its handler and start quartering before the dummy is thrown and the shot fired. The dog should then, of course, drop to the shot and mark the fall. When the judge is satisfied, it may then be sent to retrieve. The working test thus continues for however many retrieves have been arranged.

Field trials for pointer-retrievers are comparatively simple to organise, but the requirements are rather different from trials for retrievers, or for that matter for pointers and setters, or for spaniels. In retriever trials a line of guns walk up the game and the dogs in the line are expected to walk at heel and retrieve game when it is shot. In pointer and setter trials the dogs quarter the ground in pairs and find the game, pointing and backing when game is found, and honouring the flush of game by dropping. Game is not usually shot over them and if game is shot a retriever is used to retrieve it. In spaniel trials the dogs also work in pairs and are shot over, retrieving the game. In pointer-retriever trials, however, the dogs work singly and are required to quarter the ground, find game and point, honour the flush and shot and then retrieve the game. They are also expected to retrieve from, or across, water.

The pointer-retriever stakes are, as has been indicated, limited to twelve dogs since it has been found that this is as many as can usually be tested efficiently in their full role during a day. They are each run individually under two judges with anything from two to four guns in the line. They are expected to quarter their ground efficiently, find game and point, whereupon the game is shot and they are expected to retrieve. Any failure of steadiness, or failure to find game and point, or failure to retrieve satisfactorily is sufficient to put the dog out of the trial. In most cases each dog will have two, or possibly three, runs during the day if it performs well. Although a good deal of ground may be required to test the dogs fully in their role as game finders and it is also desirable to have varied ground with cover available and water to hand for the water retrieve, not a great deal of game is required. If each dog can be sure of having two points and two retrieves that should be sufficient for the judges purposes.

In an ordinary pointer-retriever trial there will usually be from two to four guns in the line, who should be good shots accustomed to shooting over pointer-retrievers, or at least over pointing dogs. If this is not the case the guns are often hypnotised by their first sight of pointing dogs and are liable to take their shots far too close and miss as a result. It is preferable to have four guns, two on each side of the handler, if there is any doubt about their abilities, since there is nothing more irritating for a handler than seeing his dog's chances reduced by a bird being missed when the dog has found the game and pointed it well. In the same way it is not desirable to have game, especially ground game, merely wounded. Although a runner well retrieved can give a dog every chance of securing a place in any trial a wounded hare, or rabbit, in front of the dog is a very strong test of steadiness and no handler will wish to have a retrieve of this nature in a trial. In such a case the judges will in any event usually ask the gun to finish it off with a second shot as a matter of plain humanity as much as anything else.

Before the start of the trial the judges should brief the guns as to what they want shot and in what circumstances. In a novice trial they may not want ground game shot. In both novice and open trials they will probably not want game shot while a dog is retrieving, although in an open trial especially in the second round, or where game is scarce and retrieves are required they might waive this edict. Normally game will not be shot unless pointed in a novice trial, although this is not necessarily the case in an open trial. Where more than one bird has been shot after a point a dog may be brought in for an unseen retrieve in either novice or open trials. Where a runner is not quickly retrieved the first dog down may be withdrawn and a second dog set on the line. The same procedure is followed wherever a dog fails to retrieve after being given reasonable time to do so.

The line at a pointer-retriever trial should thus consist of the handler with the dog that is to work, the two judges just behind him, and the guns on either side of them. The guns should spread out a good thirty yards (27.4 m) each side of the handler, or more, so that the dog quartering some fifty yards (45.7 m) each way is suitably covered. In addition, close behind the judges should be the field trial organiser, or chief steward, and the head keeper, or owner of the ground, ready to advise on which beats to take next and where game is most likely to be found. The field trial organiser, or chief steward, should be there to consult with the judges as to their requirements and to assist them in any way necessary. Some fifty yards (45.7 m) behind the line there should be another steward, or official, with the next competitor and dog ready to come up when beckoned forward by the organiser, after the judges have pronounced themselves finished with the dog they have been watching. This arrangement can save valuable time, which is always important in any field trial, but especially so in the shorter winter days.

Some fifty yards (45.7 m) or so further back should be the spectators behind the steward of the beat armed with a red flag. In many ways this is one of the more important officials since it is desirable that the spectators and other competitors should have as clear a view of the proceedings as possible, but at the same time they should not be too close. They should also be kept together and kept quiet. There is nothing more irritating for competitors working their dogs, or for the judges, to hear the sound of noisy conversation close behind them disturbing their concentration and also disturbing game. It is also, of course, highly important to make sure that no one strays away and ends up trespassing on neighbouring ground, or disturbing beats that have not yet been covered.

The draw having taken place, as is customary, when the

entries have all been accepted, the competitors will, of course, all know their order of running and will each be wearing their appropriate armbands by which the judges can identify them. For the first round they will run in the order one to twelve and take the luck of the draw as to how this affects their chances. In the second round the judges will decide in what order they want the dogs to run. This will be decided on factors involved in the first run the dog had. Thus one or more dogs may not have had a retrieve, or others for one reason or another may not have had a point. Yet others may have been unfortunate enough to run without either a point, or a retrieve, through no fault of their own.

It is, within limits, up to the judges to run the trial as they wish, for they have the authority of the Kennel Club behind them. They are appointed, it must be appreciated, by the Kennel Club and invited to judge by the club sponsoring the trial which is run under Kennel Club rules and regulations. Their decisions are final. On the other hand the chief steward, or field trial organiser, should always be ready to bring any points to their notice that he, or she, feels they might have overlooked and it is on this official that a great deal of the success of the day also depends.

Having had the ground shown to them by the head keeper, or owner, it is then up to the judges to decide how to allocate it to the competitors. Each handler must have a specific beat pointed out at the start of the run, The ground to be covered should be clearly defined, as should be the direction that is to be taken, with some instruction such as: 'Take the line of that beacon. Quarter as far as that hedge on the left and cover the guns on the right.' If the handler shows signs of straying from the line that has been set, or of not covering the entire beat correctly, this should be pointed out by one of the judges.

Although a dog may start raggedly and take a little while to settle down, especially in novice trials, the judges will usually take this into account. It is normally desirable, if possible, to give each dog a good run to start with, allowing it time to settle down and quarter its ground steadily, but, of course much depends on the ground and the circumstances. If the dog has a long run in the open without any game being seen, or missed, it may then be necessary to pick it up and bring on the next dog as it is undesirable to spend too long with any one competitor. That handler and dog will, of course, be marked down for a run later when all have had their first opportunity. The same might be true of a dog which almost immediately gets a point and retrieve, for it is always preferable to get through all twelve dogs within a reasonable time, thus giving each as a fair a chance of showing its paces as early on as possible. They may then have a second run later, and possibly even a third, or sometimes a decider after that, prior to the water retrieve.

The water retrieve is usually the last item of the day. By then there may be very little to choose betweeen one or two of the better dogs and this can have a decisive influence. It is usually carried out on a river, or suitable pond, where dead pigeons, or game shot during the day, may either be thrown into the water for a novice trial, or placed on the far bank in an open trial. The object is primarily to test the dogs as water dogs, to ensure they will enter water and swim readily, but primary objectives are sometimes forgotten by those who are keen on such tests. Since it is an artificial test, however, in my view not too great attention should be paid to it if a dog has performed creditably in the field otherwise.

The system of marking a pointer-retriever trial may vary with the judges. It is important to mark each dog on each of its runs for quartering, pointing and retrieving ability. If each is marked on these with points for nose, style and steadiness, with nose being marked out of ten and style and steadiess each out of five, the results should be easily sorted out after each round. If a dog is noted as not having had sufficient opportunity for either quartering, pointing or retrieving it may be given a further run.

A very much more complex system of marking involving a great many more items and with a system of weighting that requires a calculator to work out at the end of the day has also been widely practiced. Based on the German system it is supposed to provide more uniform results, but, of course no system is any better than the people who use it. No judge worth his, or her, salt is going to allow a marking system to decide for itself which dog should be placed first after having formed a clear idea of which are the prizewinning dogs. If any judges are prepared to accept this system without weighting it according to the views they may have formed, they are less than human, or else not fit to judge in the first place.

It is possible on a perfect scenting day to go through the twelve dogs for the first time and form a very clear picture of which are likely to be amongst the first four. On the other hand in the second round one or two may suddenly excel on a runner, or otherwise distinguish themselves and the whole picture is reversed. Alternatively in the second round the dogs which first distinguished themselves may run badly, or even be eliminated, or a dog which had no real opportunity in the first round may run very well and eventually win the trial. Where the scenting conditions are bad the chances of something on these lines happening are much greater. This is the fascination of field trials, as so much depends on the luck of the day.

When the scenting conditions are extremely bad and where game is scarce the judging of a pointer-retriever trial has special difficulties. Each dog has to have an opportunity to point and retrieve, or clearly there is not enough game to judge the trial properly, in which circumstances it would have to be declared void, although this is a step no judge would willingly take if it could be avoided. Where there is only just sufficient game, however, it may be that no dog distinguished itself well and the judges may then, at their discretion, decide not to award a first prize. In such conditions, of course, the standard of the guns is of considerable importance for if any of the few points achieved results in no retrieve the judges may find themselves in very great difficulty. In these circumstances much may depend on the water retrieve, although this is an undesirable state of affairs.

The water retrieve itself is something the judges are advised to study carefully. They should insist, where possible, in freshly shot birds and a reasonably simple entrance to and exit from the water. There is no point in making the final most artificial part of the day too difficult. The aim is to test the dogs on their ability to enter water and swim as far as possible as if it was a shooting day, not just another working test.

The water retrieve usually takes place towards the end of a long cold day when the conditions are not conducive to activity of this sort. Were it a genuine duck flighting expedition the dogs' reactions might be very different, but looking at it from their viewpoint they have probably spent a dull day on the lead with remarkably little real action and they are bored, stiff and eager to get home. Then they are suddenly expected to cross an uninviting stretch of water to fetch an unseen retrieve which frequently turns out to be a deep frozen, half thawed, pigeon. A lack of interest is understandable in the circumstances and should not be too heavily penalised if the dog has performed well during the rest of the day and shown itself to be good in the field.

There are certain basic requirements for a successful field trial for pointer-retrievers. Firstly the ground must be suitable. This means that there must be adequate space to run the dogs and sufficient, but not too much, game of various kinds. Arable farmland with some root crops is usually very suitable, although a mixture of arable land and grass may be even better, if there is a certain amount of game on it. In many ways, however, marginal land may prove better still, such as the edge of moorland, especially where there is very varied game and also an occasional sprinkling of cover. If there are suitable patches of gorse, or nettles and brambles, available to test the dogs so much the better. There should also be a river, or suitable lake, available for the water retrieve. The field trial organiser should be efficient and either he or members of the field trial committee should have inspected and approved the ground beforehand, establishing good relations with the land owner and his head keeper.

The judges should not only understand dogs and the ways of game, but also the ways of field trial competitors. Their aim should be to assess the abilities of the dogs and mark these accordingly, rather than observe their faults and mark them down, which is the easy option. They should also try to ensure an enjoyable day for everyone, for it is they who set the general tone of the proceedings. The competitors ought to be sporting or they would not be entering, but they should accept the judges' decisions, whether they agree with them or not, without complaints or ungenerous comments about others. Last, but not least, the guns should be good shots with an interest in dogs. With that combination, even in poor scenting conditions, everyone should have a good day and the dogs should be thoroughly tested, with the best dog on the day winning first prize and seen by all to deserve it. This is not as uncommon as it might sound.

There is no real reason why working tests could not be closer to field trials. Although it has not been done, as far as I know, there is no reason why good working tests for pointer-retrievers should not be held in the spring on mating pairs of partridges, when they tend to sit comparatively tight, or on grouse in early August before the season opens in the same way that some setter and pointer trials are held at those times. Such working tests could be run in exactly the same way as a normal pointer-retriever field trial with only one, or two, guns in the line and the addition of one, or two, stewards with a supply of dead pigeons. The dogs could be run one at a time, quarter their ground, find game and come on point. When the game was then flushed a blank shot could be fired and a dead bird thrown in the appropriate direction by the nearest steward to provide a realistic retrieve. The dogs could thus be judged very nearly as for an ordinary trial. The only difficulty likely to be encountered would be the normal one of obtaining ground, but there should be little real objection to such working tests in February and March, when hare shooting is still continuing, or even as later as April before the birds are nesting.

Nor is there any real objection to resuscitating the old Georgian custom of a wager between two gentlemen as to who could shoot most over their dog in a given period over a given area of ground. This rather amusing forerunner of the field trial was a purely competitive wager. Each gentleman would set out, with an umpire appointed by his opponent supervising the timing and fairness of his proceedings. Each would then shoot for whatever time had been decided on over his dog and the one who produced the largest bag won the day. Each would be followed by an interested gallery of spectators and side bets on the result would sometimes be considerable. The principle is not without its attractions even today.

The difference between controlling a dog when shooting over

it and when working it without a gun in a field trial is, of course, very considerable. The competitor in the field trial can concentrate all his, or her, attention on the dog. Although not allowed to carry any stick, or lead, the competitor has both hands free to direct the dog. The whistle can be blown at the same time as the dog is directed with the free hand, which, is difficult, to say the least, when carrying a gun. If wished, although it is never a very desirable spectacle, the handler can crouch and receive the retrieve with both hands to ensure that it is not dropped. Since this gives the appearance, rightly or wrongly, of not trusting the dog it is inclined to give the judges a poor impression and is therefore probably better avoided. Style and finish in the handler can sometimes be as important as in the dog when it comes to winning field trials. Perfect harmony and confidence between dog and handler is always a pleasure to watch and contributes to winning field trials.

The cardinal sin that a handler in a pointer-retriever trial should always avoid if possible is not getting right up on the dog when it comes on point. At the first sign that the dog has scented game and is coming on point it is advisable, however staunch and steady the dog may be, to get right up on him. The handler is then in a much better position to control the slightest sign of unsteadiness and it should be appreciated that however staunch and steady the dog may normally be to flush of game the unnatural pressures of a field trial can easily cause a breakdown of discipline even in the best of dogs. This is, of course, especially so if the handler is attempting to keep control of the dog from forty yards (36.6 m) rather than two.

The novice competitor in pointer-retriever trials will generally find there is nothing very difficult about them. If he, or she, has previously entered working tests the field trial may well seem less difficult. The judges will no doubt assemble the competitors at the start and outline what they may expect in the way of game being shot over them and will probably wish them all well. Once their turn has come it is a question of casting the dog off and quartering the beat that has been given, making sure it is fully covered and making full use of the wind.

When the dog shows signs of scenting game the handler

should close right up to maintain control and indicate that there is a point. When the judge gives the word the handler may then command the dog to flush the game and ensure it remains steady. The shot game should be marked by both dog and handler and when the judges are ready the dog may be sent to fetch it. Once the game has been retrieved to hand it should be given to the judges to inspect. If they consider there is any trace of hard mouth it will be given back to the handler to examine and pass to the steward. If all has gone well there will then be at least one more run and finally the water retrieve. After that the handler may hope to be amongst the award winners at the prizegiving.

It is, however, never worth trying to hoodwink the judges if they are reasonably experienced. A female judge may remember competing in her first trial when I was judging. She dramatically indicated her dog on point, ignoring the fact that her leg was firmly placed in front of his nose, between it and the sitting bird. She was asked to step back. The dog then dived in and unfortunately pegged the bird against a nearby fence, thus disqualifying itself. No doubt now she would still say it was a good try. Of course, if the judges do not get up in time to see what has been happening and are unwise enough to enquire from the competitor, as has been known, they are hardly likely to get an answer that will incriminate the dog. While competing in pointer-retriever trials may be nerve wracking at times, judging can be strenuous and also has its problems.

In other countries, naturally enough, the methods of running pointer-retriever trials vary considerably as do the methods of shooting. In Germany and most European countries the pointer-retriever trials are very thorough and the dogs are run for some ten minutes at least, although given an initial minute to settle down, when they are not marked. They are tested for pointing, particularly for nose, but they are allowed to run in to flush and shot, as long as they can be controlled and stopped within certain limits. They are then sent to retrieve and again marked highly for nose. The water retrieve is very testing, being usually conducted on a lake with large reed beds on a duck with the flight feathers removed and a penknife incision made in the leg to provide a blood trail. Once the duck has taken refuge in the reed beds this is of course a very difficult retrieve similar to that on a wing-tipped bird, but this would be illegal in Britain.

In the the U.S.A. there is a division between what are termed bird dogs and meat dogs. Pointer-retrievers running as bird dogs are expected to quarter the ground very wide and so fast that the judges have to keep up with them on horseback. The meat dog trials, so descriptively named, are very much on the lines of trials in the U.K. except that the birds are usually set out either on the morning before, or the day before, the trial. They have not been outside the pen where they were bred and are thus not likely to have the natural cunning of a wild bird. On the other hand the dogs are worked very thoroughly including a water retrieve. A dog of my breeding, appropriately named Dunpender Eros, was National German Shorthair Pointer Retrieving Champion in 1968 in Ohio, but as he had been bred and trained on wild birds over here this was perhaps not surprising.

In Australia, where pointer-retrievers are growing in popularity, they are expected to point dead game in A.K.C. approved trials, although enthusiasts run unofficial trials very much on the lines of pointer-retriever trials in the U.K. In New Zealand the trials are not yet recognised by the Kennel Club and are again run by enthusiasts amongst themselves. In both cases pointer-retrievers in the field are expected to work very much as in this country and, of course, are in their element.

The fact of the matter is that, field trials apart, the pointer-retriever is naturally worked very much in the same fashion in any country in the world. The dogs are either medium range, medium pace, pointer-retrievers, or wide-ranging, fast pointer-retrievers. Although the different breeds tend to produce one or other the truth of the matter is that most dogs will work according to the way they are taught and the sort of country they tend to work over most. It is only unfortunate that in this country there is not really a great deal of scope for wide-ranging, fast pointer-retrievers and too many are used solely for retrieving, or only as medium range, medium pace, pointer-retrievers. It cannot be repeated too often that each dog should be given as much variety in the field as possible.

While working tests and field trials are a good way of bringing a dog to a reasonable standard they should never be allowed to become an end in themselves. No pointer-retriever owner should ever lose sight of the fact that the dog is intended for work in the field. Unless it can work well in the field using its own initiative and instincts while working in harmony with its handler it is not fulfilling its purpose in life. Too much control of the dog, especially where the handler is not fully experienced in the ways of game, can lead to the dog being thwarted and failing to achieve its potential. Too often at field trials a dog is seen to be aware of game in front when the handler, frightened of losing control, or not reading his dog's reactions correctly, calls it back, although left to itself the dog would almost certainly have found the game and pointed it. When shooting over a dog such behaviour would merely mean an empty bag and a poor day. A few outings of this nature would soon teach the handler to have more faith in the dog, but it is precisely this experience which, of course, is lacking.

It is probable that in the U.K. the concentration on obedience in field trials is slightly overdone. The principle in Germany, whereby the dog is allowed to run in for a short distance, has the advantage that the dog's instinct is not stifled to the same extent. Anyone shooting regularly over their dog by themselves, or in the company of a few friends, will not mind greatly if the dog runs into fall, especially if there is any doubt about a bird being stone dead. It is always preferable in the field to have a runner in the bag, rather than wait and possibly lose the bird altogether. In practice, as long as the dog has been trained to the required standard and can be brought back to it when required no shooting man is likely to object to such displays of initiative in the field. When it comes to a driven shoot, or walking up in line, it is another matter, but then the dog will be working in a different manner and with experience should readily come to differentiate between the two forms of shooting.

It should again be emphasised that whether the dog has been performing in a field trial, or has been out shooting in one form or another, the handler should always look after it at the end of the day. If the dog is wet it should be dried off, not left to dry gradually in the back of the car. It should be taught to roll over on command so that the handler may easily check it over for small cuts, stakes, or gashes from barbed wire. If there are any needing attention then they should be treated as soon as possible, not left for the return home, or the following day. If stitches are required the dog should be taken to the vet at once. The dog should also be watered, fed and bedded down comfortably as soon as the handler returns home. A good dog is worth these minimal attentions but far too few receive them.

Let those who do leave their dog undried and uncared for in the back of their car at least take heed. I have known dogs of several breeds left in such circumstances, including one retriever field trial champion, which were found, on their owner's belated return, to be sitting surrounded by blood and feathers having consumed the brace of birds their owner had left in the car with them. The retriever in question was actually half way through a very large hare, but in the circumstances who can blame the dogs?

Whether the trainer owns a medium range, medium pace, pointer-retriever, or a wide-ranging, fast pointer-retriever, or has managed to combine them in one dog, by the time it is trained the communication between them should be a totally unconscious affair. The dog should be attuned to the trainer and the trainer to the dog. In the field the dog will be quartering the ground using its scenting powers to the full and the trainer will be interpreting each check, or movement, without conscious thought or effort. When the trainer wishes to signal the dog to change direction, or cover some particular ground, there should be total harmony between them.

The dog has the scenting abilities on which the trainer relies and the trainer has the gun which despatches the game once the dog has found and pointed it. Thereafter the dog retrieves it as a natural extension of its part in the proceedings. The trainer then directs it onto new ground and so the day continues, each playing an important part without which the other could not be successful. In that partnership and harmony of communication and understanding lies all the interest and enjoyment of the sport. Whatever the day may hold, whether it is a full scale driven shoot, or merely a short outing by themselves, the same timeless message may be addressed to both trainer and dog:

'Good hunting'.

Glossary of Technical Terms

Air scent: scent particles carried on the air.

Back: to honour the point of another dog on sight by coming on point also.

Blink: Blinking: (Old term) can mean not remaining staunch on point and returning to the handler: can also mean failing to point game.

Bracework: two dogs working in unison: method depends on ground.

Break field: or Break fence: to enter a field without orders, in front of handler: to cross a fence without orders.

Clap down: Clapped: of game, squatting, frozen to avoid danger: will often remain thus in front of dog on point.

Clean delivery: the presentation of game to the handler by the dog without mouthing, or fuss.

Cheeper: young game bird so-called after noise emitted in flight.

Draw on: of dog, to advance steadily towards game while on point.

False point: a point made where no game lies.

Flush: to cause game to take flight, or break from cover.

Foot scent: or Ground scent: scent particles left on the ground by the feet of the game.

Fur, or feather: ground game, or game birds.

Ground game: Rabbits and hares.

Heel scent: the track leading away from game, often followed by inexperienced dog.

Hide: small artificially constructed place of concealment, from which to shoot pigeons, or wildfowl.

Honour flush: or Acknowledge flush: to drop to flushed game.

Honour point: to back the point of another dog.

Long drop: when the dog sits, or drops, at a distance to whistle, signal, or command it is so described.

Losing its nose: if dog confused by too much or too strong a scent. Unable to scent anything as a result, e.g. dog fed strong cheese, or in a pheasant pen.

Nose: of dog, scenting ability: hunting dog's greatest attribute.

Peg or seize: game lying 'clapped'.

Pottering: of dog, lacking pace and failing to cover ground adequately: may be due to age, or physical infirmity, or to lack of nose.

Reading the dog: to interpret each of the dog's actions correctly while it is quartering, or hunting, or otherwise working.

Road out: to work out a scent after game has been flushed to ensure that it has all gone.

Runner: a bird which has been shot, generally in the wing, but is capable of running, often for considerable distances and at considerable speed.

Self-hunting: the act of a gundog going off hunting in the hedgerows, or fields, for game: a very bad vice which can lead to sheep worrying: it should never be allowed: but it is extremely hard to cure once started.

Spurs: the claws of a cock pheasant.

Sticky: of pointing dog, which will not move forward without very considerable persuasion because so firmly and rigidly on point: usually a sign of immaturity.

Swing: to move the gun across the body at speed after a crossing bird.

Using wind correctly: working into the wind so that the scent particles from the game are coming to dog, rather than downwind when the scent particles are blown from the working dog towards the waiting game.

Index